Social Work and Mental Health

THIRD EDITION

MALCOLM GOLIGHTLEY

Series Editors: Jonathan Parker and Greta Bradley

LearningMatters

First published in 2004 by Learning Matters Ltd.
Reprinted twice in 2005
Second edition published in 2006
Third edition published in 2008

British Library Cataloguing in Publication Data
A CIP record for this book is available from the British Library.

ISBN-13: 978 1 84445 154 8

Cover and text design by Code 5 Design Associates
Project management by Deer Park Productions
Typeset by Pantek Arts Ltd, Kent
Printed and bound in Great Britain by Cromwell Press Ltd, Trowbridge, Wiltshire

Learning Matters Ltd
33 Southernhay East
Exeter EX1 1NX
Tel: 01392 215560
info@learningmatters.co.uk
www.learningmatters.co.uk

362.2
GOL

DATE DUE

Transforming Social Work Practice – titles in the series

To order, please contact our distributor: BEBC Distribution, Albion Close, Parkstone, Poole, BH12 3LL. Telephone: 0845 230 9000, email: learningmatters@bebc.co.uk. You can also find more information on each of these titles and our other learning resources at www.learningmatters.co.uk.

Contents

Acknowledgements

Thanks are due to the countless people who over the years have maintained my interest in mental health. These have been professionals, volunteers, carers and service users. More specifically thanks are due to Professor Bob Peckitt, consultant psychiatrist for advice and guidance for Chapter 2; Christopher Curran, a fellow of the University of Lincoln, and David Hewitt, a solicitor and Fellow of the University for their considerable expertise and support to help me to unravel the new legislation. Colleagues Mike Ogley and Jim Rogers have given their advice and proofreading services. The popularity of earlier additions has been as encouraging as it has been a surprise and a special thanks needs to go to all those students whose praise for the book has been heartwarming.

These days life in Higher Education is very full and pressured. There is no spare capacity so writing a book like this not only demands much of one's personal time but of course has an effect on everyone at work. My colleagues at the University of Lincoln deserve many thanks for their support and tolerance.

This book has been a long time in the making but has allowed me to indulge myself in an area which I am passionate about and have been involved in for over 20 years as a practitioner, academic, researcher, and user and carer. I hope the contents do justice to the richness of the experience and to all the things that I have learned from service users and other influential people.

This book is dedicated to Pam, our family, Sharada, Rosie, Sarah, Liam and my grandchildren Kezie Harrison, Maddison Rose and Holly May.

List of Abbreviations

AC	approved clinician
AMHP	approved mental health professional
ASW	approved social worker; to be replaced by the AMHP
BASW	British Association of Social Workers
BMA	British Medical Association
BNF	British National Formulary
CAMHS	child and adolescent mental health services
CBT	cognitive behavioural therapy
CMHT	community mental health team
CPA	care programme approach
CPN	community psychiatric nurse
CTO	community treatment order
DoH	Department of Health
DoLS	deprivation of liberty safeguards
EC	European Commission
ECT	electroconvulsive therapy
EE	expressed emotion
GP	general practitioner
MDO	mentally disordered offender
MHAC	Mental Health Act Commission
MHRT	Mental Health Review Tribunal
NHS	National Health Service
NMC	Nursing and Midwifery Council
NR	nearest relative (legal term)
OT	occupational therapist
PHCT	primary health care team
RMO	responsible medical officer (1983 MHA); now replaced by the RC
RC	responsible clinician
SCT	supervised community treatment
SOAD	second opinion appointed doctor
SSRI	selective serotonin reuptake inhibitor
WHO	World Health Organisation

Introduction

This third edition is written primarily for student social workers who are studying for their professional qualification. This third edition was needed as finally the government has introduced a new act to amend the provisions of the existing legislation. The 2007 Mental Health Act will probably be fully enacted in 2008 and brings with it some important and very significant changes. Whilst it is aimed at first or second year students it will also be useful for the final year and professional practice. The book will appeal to those who work with social workers in the mental health field and to those who are studying related qualifications such as the Certificate in Community Mental Health Care. Experienced and qualified workers should find the content useful for professional updating and to help them understand what students on the new degree are studying.

Requirements for social work education

This book will help students to meet the demands outlined by the Department of Health in the prescribed curriculum and especially in relation to the expressed need that all social workers must understand about mental health and how to work with colleagues from other disciplines.

It will also help students to meet the new social work subject benchmarks published in April 2008 by the Quality Assurance Agency for Higher Education. These are incorporated at the start of each chapter. These include being able to understand the nature of social work and developing knowledge and understanding about the following:

- social work services and service users;

- values and ethics;

- social work theory; and

- the nature of social work practice.

The National Occupational Standards set for social workers are also covered as the book examines the roles that social workers must play if change and development are to be achieved at an individual, group and service level.

Book structure

Mental health services are in a state of continual change. After a long wait and considerable debate we haven't a totally new law but in the 2007 Mental Health Act a major and substantial amendment to the 1983 Mental Health Act. With the accompanying changes to the Mental Capacity Act and the two new Codes of Practice we are entering into a new way of working which will make the next few years both interesting and challenging. Meanwhile new government policies have come into being that will affect both adult services and children and young people services. Although integrated services are high on this agenda it remains my view that social work should be at the heart of these changes and a crucial part of delivering improved services for vulnerable people. This book has in its own modest way a part to play in the transformation of future social work practice.

The beginning of the book has a clear focus upon values and the importance of social workers underpinning their practice with values and principles that demonstrate that they can work with diverse populations, some of whom experience disadvantage and oppression. The examples of work with black and minority ethnic communities and people who are deaf serve to demonstrate the necessity for culturally sensitive practice.

In Chapter 2 the medical model is described in detail as this is the dominant approach to work with service users. However it is not the only approach and the case is put that a more socially oriented approach needs to be understood by social workers as well as the medical approach. This orientation is about more than providing services to support medical interventions: it takes into account a more holistic view of the confusing and contradictory world of mental disorder. To help understand this emphasis is placed on the role that stress has as an intervening variable that increases the vulnerability of people to mental disorder. Such stressful events can include life events or circumstances such as unemployment or relationship breakdown.

The law is never far from mental health social work and Chapter 3 examines the new legal and political context in which social workers, approved social workers and the approved mental health worker will find themselves. The case for and against compulsory admission is made and the process covered. Emphasis is placed on human rights and how they are incorporated into the legislation, and how the various community care initiatives can allow imaginative solutions for helping people return to or remain in the community. The main provisions refer only to the law in England.

Chapter 4 examines work with children and adolescents at a time when *Every Child Matters* has recently come into play and children and young people's services will be altered out of all recognition. Even so, social workers will continue to be among those who will work with a range of mental health disorders that children and young people face. The Child and Adolescent Mental Health Service is a relatively new response and, although slow to get underway, is for the foreseeable future what services will look like. The example of eating disorder is covered in some detail to provide an example of work with adolescents.

Working with service users who are short-term users of mental health services provides the content of Chapter 5. In particular the task facing social workers who are working with people who are at risk of suicide provides the subject matter, with an illustrative example that runs throughout most of the chapter. The importance of understanding the research evidence that frames our work in any area is given emphasis.

Chapter 6 looks at work with service users who have long-term or chronic needs. The illustrative example of a man diagnosed with schizophrenia is used and in particular the concept of early intervention and family work are suggested as ways that effective intervention can be accomplished. Stressful situations can include families that have 'high expressed emotion' and this is used to demonstrate effective work with families. The differences in diagnosis between Afro-Caribbean young men and their white counterparts are explored, and the concept of risk is briefly examined.

The final chapter returns the reader to work with children and the concept of working across professional and organisational boundaries. This covers the importance of child protection and the case of Victoria Climbié. Learning lessons from Inquiries includes learning how to work better together – the Allitt Inquiry raises important issues of which social work professionals should be aware. Children whose parents separate can respond adversely to the stresses that this event can create. Yet others get by and even thrive in later life, and their resilience and ability to bounce back is considered in detail as it provides an important series of pointers as to where intervention could be targeted.

Finally some signposts for the future are aired during the last few pages.

Learning features

As far as a book can be, this has been written to help you to interact with the material as an active participant. The combination of this book, liberal use of the internet and self-reflection should ensure effective learning.

Case studies are used throughout the book to help make real the application of the theory to practice. To add interest some historical notes are provided, especially in Chapter 3.

Throughout this book stress is seen as something that can tip someone from being mentally healthy into having a mental health problem. This can be a single event although often it is a build-up of little things. These need to be dealt with and some chapters provide tips to bust your stress.

Chapter 1

Values and ethical mental health social work

ACHIEVING A SOCIAL WORK DEGREE

National Occupational Standards are competence statements that are used to describe good professional practice. They describe what service users should expect the professional to be like. They help to describe the link between the aims and objectives of an organisation and what individual workers need to be able to achieve (Skills for Health, 2003). To help you to understand your own level of knowledge, understanding and skills you can use National Occupational Standards and they will help you to identify any deficit in these areas (see TOPSS website: www.toppss.org.uk).

Key Role 1: Prepare for and work with individuals, families, carers, groups and communities to assess their needs and circumstances

Key Role 2: Plan, carry out, review and evaluate social work practice, with individuals, families, carers, groups and communities and other professionals

It will also introduce you to the following academic standards as set out in the social work benchmark statement which includes:

5.1.1 Social work services and service users

- The social work processes (associated with, for example, poverty, unemployment, poor health, disablement, lack of education and other sources of disadvantage) that lead to marginalisation, isolation and exclusion and their impact on the demand for social work services.
- Explanations of the links between definitional processes contributing to social differences (for example, social class, gender and ethnic differences) to the problems of inequality and differential need faced by service users.
- The nature of social work services in a diverse society (with particular reference to concepts such as prejudice, interpersonal, institutional and structural discrimination, empowerment and anti-discriminatory practices).

5.1.3 Values and ethics, which include

- The moral concepts of rights, responsibility, freedom, authority and power inherent in the practice of social workers as moral and statutory agents.
- The complex relationships between justice, care and control in social welfare and the practical and ethical implications of these, including roles as statutory agents and in upholding the law in respect of discrimination.
- The conceptual links between codes defining ethical practice, the regulation of professional conduct and the management of potential conflicts generated by the codes held by different professional groups.
- Aspects of philosophical ethics relevant to the understanding and resolution of value dilemmas and conflicts in both interpersonal and professional contexts.

Introduction

The World Heath Organisation describes **mental health** as:

> *a state of well-being in which the individual realizes his or her abilities, can cope with the normal stresses of life, can work productively and fruitfully, and is able to make a contribution to his or her community.*

> *MENTAL ill health includes mental health problems and strain, impaired functioning associated with distress, symptoms, and diagnosable mental health disorders, such as schizophrenia and depression.*

> *The mental condition of people is determined by a multiplicity of factors including biological, individual, family and social, economic and environmental.*
> (European Commission Green Paper, 2005, p.4)

This chapter examines the relationship between values, ethics, contemporary social work and social care practice in the Mental Health Services. Mental health services are at a crucial stage of redevelopment which, by the time it is complete, will produce a service that is appropriate and responsive to service user needs. Values and ethics are at the heart of culturally competent professional practice. This means that social workers will be able to value their own culture and be able to work in a sensitive manner with people from other cultures. To become culturally competent requires empathy, understanding and acceptance of differences. (Walker, 2003; see also culturally sensitive practice in *Engaging and Changing*, Patel, 2003).

Approximately one person in six, at some time in their life, will experience mental health problems that are sufficiently serious for them to seek help from a professional. It is usually the family doctor who is the first port of call and they in turn refer people on to the various agencies whose remit is to provide mental health services. These services include health, social care and social work agencies that are trying to work together to provide a seamless service for the user. Some GP practices have social workers attached to them and this often means that these workers will be doing direct work with service users, working in the community alongside other mental health professionals, or be working in a psychiatric hospital. Social workers also come across mental health problems in addition to the 'presenting problem' that led to referral in the first place.

A strategy for the mental health of the European Union

In January 2005 the World Health Organisation held a conference for European Ministers to start a process of drawing up a framework for comprehensive action and political commitment for mental health. The subsequent Green Paper is an important contribution to setting up a series of actions that may prove to be a significant initiative. The purpose of the Green Paper is to stimulate debate within Europe and to engage a broad range of institutions, health professionals, social care professionals, research communities and service users, in discussions about how best to improve public mental health.

The Green Paper outlines three areas for improvement:

Mental ill health affects every fourth citizen and can lead to suicide, a cause of too many deaths.

Mental ill health causes significant losses and burdens to the economic, social, educational as well as criminal and justice systems.

Stigmatisation, discrimination and non-respect for the human rights and the dignity of mentally ill and disabled people still exist, challenging core European values.
(European Commission Green Paper, 2005)

The Paper goes on to describe how mental health is a growing challenge to the EU and to support the WHO view that by 2020 depression will be the highest ranking cause of disease in the developed world (WHO, 2001). Other statistics include the statement that:

Currently, in the EU, some 58000 citizens die from suicide every year, more than from the annual deaths from road accidents, homicide or HIV/AIDS.
(Green Paper, p.4)

Clearly there are significant inequalities within member states and this reflects the richness of the diverse nature of the EU but nevertheless the Paper proposes that a strategy would be focused upon prevention of mental ill health, the improvement of the quality of life for people with mental health and the development of a mental health information and research system for the EU.

The strategy for England and Wales

The government has set about improving mental health care in general. Key policy documents are *Modernising Mental Health Services* (Department of Health, 1998) and the NHS Plan (Department of Health, 2000). One of the key tasks for the reformed services is to combat the effects of social exclusion and to provide a service that is user-focused. The idea is that through a combination of policy initiatives people will feel that they have a greater sense of belonging to a community and services will form new partnerships between the providers and recipients of services. Thus various initiatives have been put in place to meet the needs of specific populations such as women, people who are deaf, and black and minority ethnic groups.

This more inclusive approach has a focus on community-based services which has been a trend over the last two decades. Prior to this care was provided largely through admission to hospitals, many of which were based on the outskirts of cities and towns. As patients were transferred from hospital to community the danger was that services would become more fragmented. With decentralised structures there is a need to establish general standards against which these communities' services can be judged. The Mental Health National Service Framework (DoH, 1999) is in effect a series of mission statements or targets for services. There are NSFs for mental health, older people, adults and children and young people.

The National Service Framework for adult mental health has seven standards:

- **Standard One** covers mental health promotion and aspects of discrimination and social exclusion that is associated with mental health problems.

- **Standards Two and Three** cover primary care services for people who have mental health problems and include 24-hour crisis services.

- **Standards four and five** highlight what is needed to provide effective services for people with mental health problems. This includes being familiar with the Care Programme Approach and its relation to care management.

- **Standard six** relates to the individuals who care for people with mental health problems, with Social Service Departments being given the lead responsibility in ensuring that all carers' needs are assessed and that they receive their own written care plans.

- **Standard seven** sets out what is needed to achieve a reduction in suicides. This will potentially involve all social workers in a range of settings.

These standards need to be seen alongside the more specific inspection standards such as those of the Commission for Social Care Inspection (CSCI), the successor in April 2004 to the National Care Standards Commission.

Meeting these standards is a challenge to agencies as well as to individual practitioners. As a social worker you may be working with service users and communities as well as other professionals to plan, implement and evaluate mental health services. The emphases on user empowerment, community development and non-discriminatory services are all part of the tool kit that you, as a social worker, will be expected to develop.

Before you can begin to consider yourself an effective mental health social worker you need to understand the values that underpin professional practice and how they are reflected in agency policy and practice and endorsed in governmental policies. You need to understand the part that you will play as a social worker/social care worker in the modernising agenda. It is important that as a developing professional your practice demonstrates commitment to promoting equality.

Two other key policy documents have come into place since the first edition of this book that you will need to familiarise yourself with and these are the Green Paper and the subsequent White Paper known as *Every Child Matters* and for adults the White Paper *Our Health, Our Care, Our Say*: A new direction for community services. Both these documents signal a major change in the way that the Government sees services being provided. They are both accompanied by informative and easy to access websites. As yet many of the implications are still being worked through and you as an emergent professional will be expected to not only understand these changes but also to be a part of the change dynamic.

The importance of policy

Recent policy papers

Present day life in government departments must be a dizzying experience as staff try to produce or perhaps even keep abreast of new initatives. To do so is very important for social workers and as a student you need to develop the habit of reading and critically appraising policy documents and legislation. This is the case even if at first glance such initiatives seem not to be directly related to your area of practice. I have singled out two key papers to help provide the context in which you as a social worker will practice. These are referred to later on in the book but here is a brief summary of the key points.

Our health, our care, our say: a new direction for community services (January, 2006)

This White Paper sets a new direction for the whole health and social care system in respect of adult services. It is founded on the ideas that were consulted on in the Department of Health Green Paper, **Independence, Well-being and Choice (March, 2005)**. The new direction will put service users more than ever at the centre of services which will mean that services will need to be personalised and tailored to ensure that they will fit the service users' needs. Social workers are well placed to work alongside service users to ensure that they become the drivers of service improvement.

The White Paper identifies four main goals:

1. Prevention and early intervention. This will include more support to maintain and even promote mental health and emotional well being.

2. More choice and a louder voice which will aim to provide real choice for service users on a range of services and to provide better information to enable such choices to be made.

3. Inequalities and improving access will focus upon those with ongoing needs in ethnic minorites and young people with disabilities, etc.

4. More support for people with long-term needs so that they can manage their long-term conditions out of hospital and to provide them with a clear plan to help them to promote thier own well being.

Every Child Matters

In 2003 following the death of Victoria Climbié in tragic circumstances, the Goverment published a Green Paper called *Every Child Matters* and once again the tragic circumstances surrounding a child's death and the inadequacies of services led to a major review of provision for children in general. This was aided by an excellent website which you should visit (www.everychildmatters.gov.uk)

Following the consultation, the goverment published *Every Child Matters: the Next Steps*, and passed the Children Act 2004, which set up legislation necessary for developing more effective and accessible services for children, young people and their families.

The commonly held view is that this legislation will transform the provision of services and will change the context in which services are provided irrespective of whether a child or young person has a mental illness, has emotional problems, is socially excluded or in other ways needs their well-being to be enhanced. This new direction offers up the possibility of more integrated services which are fit for purpose.

The five outcomes set out by ECM are:

- Being healthy
- Staying safe

- Enjoying and achieving
- Making a positive contribution
- Social and economic well-being.

The importance of values

Social work is fundamentally a moral activity. Social workers often refer to values, indeed Clark (2000) suggests that values are the staple diet of social workers although the word is used indiscriminately when principles or ethics would be more accurate. Clark suggest that there are four core values:

1. The worth and uniqueness of each individual.

2. The entitlement to justice.

3. The essentiality of community.

4. The claim to freedom.

These values are given statutory force through the National Health Service and Community Care Act (DoH, 1990) and various practice guidance notes including Valuing People (DoH, 2001) that stress not only the importance of these values but require services and practitioners to uphold them.

Values, knowledge and skills are interconnected in everyday practice even though this is not always apparent. Figure 1 shows how these are connected to each other.

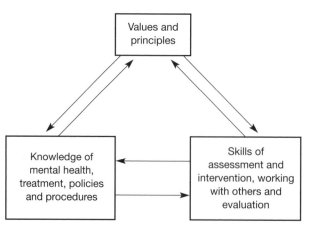

Figure 1.1 *Values, knowledge and skills: the foundations of good practice*

All social care workers will be required in the future to register with the General Social Care Council, starting in April 2005 with social workers. Once this process is complete it will allow external confirmation that a member of staff is registered and suitably qualified. This process regulates who can and who cannot enter the profession and is considered necessary in order to drive up the standards of social work and social care practice (Banks, 2000).

The need for a Code of Professional Practice becomes apparent when you begin to learn about the role that social workers have alongside other professionals who deliver mental health services. At times people with mental health problems can be in such a vulnerable state that they may even require admission to hospital against their wishes. They need to be assured that nationally agreed standards of service delivery are being adhered to and that the service provider can be held accountable when services fall short. Different professions have their own codes of practice and conduct which have three common themes:

- the avoidance of possible harm to services users;

- the promotion of possible good to service users;

- the protection of the profession and the resolution of conflicts.

How are you going to be guided by values and ethics?

The Code sets out the responsibilities for both employers and employees as follows.

Social care workers must:

- Protect the rights and promote the interests of service users and carers.

- Strive to establish and maintain the trust and confidence of service users and carers.

- Promote the independence of service users while protecting them as far as possible from danger and harm.

- Respect the rights of service users whilst seeking to ensure that their behaviour does not harm themselves or other people.

- Uphold public trust and confidence in social care services.

- Be accountable for the quality of their work and take responsibility for maintaining and improving their knowledge and skills.

ACTIVITY **1.1**

Look at your Code of Practice which sets out the kind of professional conduct and practice that is required (GSCC, 2002). You should have a copy of this Code but if not you can print it off the GSCC website or obtain a hard copy from them: General Social Care Council, Goldings House, 2 Hay's Lane, London SE1 2BH. Tel: 020 7397 5100. Email: info@gscc.org.uk www.gscc.org.uk

Make sure that you are aware of the contents of the Code.

Look at the above Code. Taking all the aspects reorder them to fit into the framework proposed earlier:

- *ones that avoid possible harm to service users;*

- *ones that promote possible good to service users;*

- *ones that protect the profession and resolve conflicts.*

Values in action

Implicit in the Code of Professional Social Work Practice is the importance of recognising and respecting diversity. This is more than valuing people irrespective of their race, colour or ability. It also involves valuing and respecting that people think and behave differently. People of all ethnic backgrounds and countries experience mental disorder and the service user population is made up of people just like you and me.

Conventionally and stereotypically medical practice has remained the dominant partner through its claim to be a series of technical activities. Advances in medication have reinforced the idea that an individual's mental disorder can be managed and that the key process is diagnosis followed by treatment monitoring and evaluation. In this process the danger is that the treated are subservient to those in charge of treatment.

Social workers need to work with medical and health colleagues to provide an effective service but they also need to be at the forefront of processes that empower service users. Implicit in this approach are some ordinary but powerful principles.

The first is that in order to empower someone we need to work with them rather than do things to them. Empowerment means partnership, openness and honesty.

The second principle is that the service user has an explanation of their disorder. That needs understanding and to achieve this we need to find ways of active listening that respect the user and enable us to do our job. This may mean having to use imaginative ways of communicating. It might mean trying to use a common language, which could be sign language. It should mean engaging in clear, uncomplicated language that everyone can understand.

The third principle is that service users value being able to engage with professionals on a personal level. This could mean that social workers should learn to use 'limited' self-disclosure to help build up professional relationships that are also person-to-person, not expert to amateur (Blackburn and Golightley, 2004). Being able to walk in the other person's shoes is an important part of an empowering approach.

The fourth principle is that the service user is the expert in their own mental health problem. They may not know the answers but they certainly experience the effect or symptoms. They alone have experienced the disintegration of 'normality' as they know it and their explanation should be put alongside the professional view and the two views evaluated against each other. If your world is upside down or inside out it cannot be understood by people who only see things one way up or right side out. If a service user is hearing voices the social worker must not dismiss these but try to understand when they arrive, what they feel like and how best they can be managed. This is not to collude with delusional behaviour as this could be unhelpful and possibly run the risk of missing dangerous behaviour.

By working with service users to value their experiences, and by seeing the problem through their eyes, the prospect is opened up to work in a manner that is holistic and empowering.

Ethical dilemmas

Health and social care workers work with dilemmas on a daily basis. There are usually two components that help us to think about ethical dilemmas. First there may be competing views about what should be done. How would you respond to a service user when they want to stop taking their medicine? This is an ethical dilemma and people would argue strongly for one position or the other. This contrasts with a view that medicine should be given with or without service user consent, if it were necessary to prevent death or serious harm occurring. In this instance this is not an ethical issue as there is widespread agreement. (Even so some people claim this should not happen, usually on religious grounds.)

The second characteristic is that it must have a distinct moral component to it, such as the avoidance of lying, the primacy of life, self-determination and confidentiality. These are sometimes referred to as 'normative principles'.

Resolving ethical dilemmas takes more than just referring to these normative principles or the various codes of conduct. It requires professional judgments after weighing up one principle against another. The following activity will help you to think further about the ethical dilemmas.

ACTIVITY **1.2**

Sanjay is a long-term service user who has recurring bouts of depression, which are serious enough to warrant his treatment with anti-depressants. In the past when his mood has been very low he has talked about 'ending it all'. As his social worker you visit regularly and he tells you in confidence that he has stopped his medication and is going to experiment with herbal medicine which is more usual in his culture. He has asked your opinion about this action and told you to keep this conversation confidential. Should you respect his wishes? Jot down what your response would be and what the issues are. Now compare with the following paragraphs.

If anyone wants to stop taking medication then this is their right under common law. In certain circumstances, and providing that they are detained under the Mental Health Act 1983, they can be made to have treatment against their wishes. Sanjay can stop his medication although whether this is a good thing is open to debate.

Arguments against keeping confidences or keeping matters confidential derive from different sources. First there is a principle of paternalism usually derived from the possession of 'expert' knowledge. Put crudely the professional knows best. Second there is a principle of autonomy where the person has freedom over his or her own body, which is essentially a moral principle. Individuals are experts in their own mental health condition and as such they know best. Resolution of this requires you to balance the strength of one principle against the other. In practice you would probably seek to encourage Sanjay to sit with the others involved in his treatment and to talk through his and your concerns and try to get to a position where his shift to herbal remedies is informed by evidence, monitored and reviewed.

You would need to take into account the extent to which the service user has the capacity to be able to make such a decision, the quality of the information on which this is based, if there was any coercion on the service user when making this decision and any legal issues that could change the nature of the discussion.

One way that service users can be helped to make good quality decisions is through patient advocacy services. By using advocates who are independent of the mental health team, but who have specific knowledge of mental health and mental health services, the quality of service user decisions can be enhanced.

Ethnicity and mental health

The discrimination that is experienced by people with mental health problems can be intensified if that person happens to be from a black and minority ethnic community. A service user talks about her experience of using mental health services as a black person:

> *Coming to mental health services was like the last straw ... you come to services disempowered already, they strip you of your dignity ... you become the dregs of society.* (Keating and Robertson, 2002, p.18)

This is a commonly held experience of black service users. When put together with the perception that when black people are seen as difficult they are likely to be over medicated there is little wonder that this has become a priority area.

Discrimination has been a source of concern to many practitioners over the years. Evidence has suggested that on the one hand the UK's black and minority ethnic population are over-represented in secondary care (hospital admissions etc) and on the other hand under-represented in primary care that specifically addresses the needs of black and minority ethnic communities. Of particular concern has been the over-representation of Caribbean and black African people who have been detained against their will and who are being treated in Medium Secure Hospitals (MSUs). Evidence collected by the Mental Health Act Commission shows that 30% of the population resident in MSUs were from predominantly black African or Caribbean ethnic groups, which is well over the proportion that might be expected when compared with the population at large.

Fundamental to developing better social work practice is having better quality of information and using it more intelligently than is evident at present. A starting point is for you to become familiar with population data and information about ethnic minorities.

ACTIVITY **1.3**

The proportion of black and minority ethnic groups in the UK rose from 6% to 9% over the period 1991–2001. The Afro-Caribbean population in England and Wales is about 2%. This does vary considerably depending on where you live and work. Commonly members of the public at large over-estimate the numbers of black and minority ethnic populations. Think about why this is, what influences this perception and what some of the implications of this might be. Write down why you think some ethnic groups are thought to be larger than they actually, are, what influences this perception and some of the implications of this.

You probably came up with the idea that the media plays a big role here with some of the less sophisticated newspapers in particular promoting the idea that we are being overpopulated with asylum seekers, drug users and the like. Mental health is not the only area where we see statistics that ought to concern us: the *Sunday Times* (Dec 14, 2003) reported, 'twice as many black people are in prison as at university'. They report that the Race Relations watchdog has concluded that while 10,000 Afro-Caribbeans are in jails – a much higher percentage than to be expected – the numbers at university are only about 5,000.

Providing mental health services that are, and need to be seen to be, responsive to the needs of individuals requires that they should reflect the rich diversity that makes up our society. However in the late 1980s it was becoming apparent that although moves were being made to promote patient-centred services this did nothing to address the specific needs of the black and minority ethnic communities.

Although these views were commonly held throughout health and social care, social work was one of the few professions that placed special emphasis on training in anti-racist and anti-discriminatory practice. At the policy level, the government's Modernisation Plan and the Mental Health National Service Framework (1999) sets out in Standard One the need to combat discrimination against individuals and groups with mental health problems and promote their social inclusion. This has built on the legal foundation laid down in the Human Rights Act 1998 and is given extra strength by the introduction of the Race Relations (Amendment) Act 2000.

More recently the Department of Health has set out an impressive and ambitious change agenda called *Delivering Race Equality: A Framework for Action* (October 2003). Although this is a consultation document, and may be amended, it is likely that the general approach and principles will remain.

What does this mean for mental health social work practice?

James Nazroo (1999) suggests that different rates of diagnosis of mental illness between black and minority ethnic people represents one of the most controversial issues that present day services face. In practical terms you need to examine the reasons why minority groups such as Afro-Caribbean men are six times more likely to be compulsorily detained than white people, why Asian women are more likely to be depressed than their white counterparts and why minority ethnic groups are less likely to seek early help from primary care.

Mental health is a significant area of social work practice, which will bring you face to face with people who may be vulnerable and confused. As a social worker you need to work together with other professionals in a way that is person-centred and upholds human rights. This is far from straightforward, with tension and conflict possible at virtually every stage of your work. Such tension can exist between for example:

- the wishes of the service user and their families;
- the need to protect the public and the need to promote service user independence;
- and, as you saw earlier, the right to refuse treatment and the need to have treatment.

In trying to work with these tensions you will often find yourself playing a crucial role in any decision-making context.

Anti-oppressive practice

Social work has a history of attempts to practise in ways that are anti-oppressive. One of the key figures in the literature is Dominelli whose book *Anti-Racist Social Work* (1988) not only provides well argued discussion about these issues but also gives strategies for the implementation of anti-racist social work. These ideas, although nearly two decades old, still have relevance for you as a practitioner as mental health care is the only aspect of care provision and treatment that, if refused, can result in that person's compulsory admission to hospital through a legally authorised pathway. Social workers, after suitable post-qualifying training, can be a major part of such procedures and can also be involved in other aspects such as providing advocacy, reports for tribunals, arranging diversion into community resources, etc.

ACTIVITY 1.4

Think of a situation where, in practical terms, you will have to take culture into account when working with someone from a black and minority ethnic background.

There will be lots of examples that you could give and one is when compiling a Social Circumstances Report for a Mental Health Review Tribunal. Tribunals take place when someone has been detained in a psychiatric facility and wishes to appeal against this detention. The Tribunals consider various reports including ones compiled by social workers. These are formal reports that are presented to the Tribunal and they are a part of the mechanism by which compulsorily detained patients can be discharged from hospital. These reports provide the Tribunal with the cultural background of the service user and describe past patterns of behaviour that can help to determine the likely success of aftercare, together with other salient details such as accommodation and employment opportunities.

The Mental Health Act Code of Practice sets out as a guiding principle that all people should be respected for their:

> ... *diverse backgrounds as individuals and be assured that account will be taken of their age, gender, sexual orientation, social, ethnic, cultural and religious background, but that general assumptions will not be made on the basis of any one of these characteristics.*
> (DoH, 1999, p.3)

This latter point is especially relevant as there is a risk of assuming cultural stereotypes, which can not only cause offence but can be widely misleading. In any event understanding someone's culture is only a first step towards anti-oppressive practice.

Are black and minority ethnic people the only community who get poorer services than the majority population? The answer is a qualified no! Other groups include older people, children and adolescents, women and people who are deaf. All these groups are covered in this book but working with mental health users who are deaf raises some interesting parallels with working with black and minority ethnic users as well as some challenges for you to face in your practice.

Deaf people and mental health

CASE STUDY

There are limited specialist services available for deaf people who have severe mental illness. This was highlighted by the Independent Inquiry into the care and treatment of Daniel Joseph (Mischoh, 2000), which was commissioned by some of the London Health Authorities. Daniel was profoundly deaf and was admitted to hospital from the courts having been made subject to a hospital order with restrictions after pleading guilty to manslaughter with diminished responsibility. Concern over his treatment resulted in the present government consulting about services across the spectrum for service users who are deaf.

People who are deaf, like black and minority ethnic people, report that mental health services are difficult to access and often do not cater for their specific needs. To raise our awareness of the specific needs of minority communities the Department of Health consultation paper *A Sign of the Times: Modernising mental health services for people who are deaf* (DoH, 2002) is worth consulting. Developing awareness of specific communities is an important, but only a first, step towards developing appropriate and responsive services.

The Royal National Institute for Deaf People estimates that there are eight million people who suffer from hearing loss, often associated with aging, and that there are about 50,000 people for whom British Sign Language is their first and preferred language (RNID, 2003).

Members of the deaf community experience mental health problems just like people from any other community. However because of the difference in language and culture between those who are assessing deaf service users and the service users themselves, misdiagnosis can result and as a consequence deaf people can receive services and treatment that are inappropriate. Good practice needs to take into consideration the requirements of the Disability Discrimination Act (DoH,1999) which makes it clear that mental health services have to take reasonable steps to facilitate the uptake of services by people who are deaf and who have mental health problems (sometimes referred to as people with dual diagnosis). This includes the use of an interpreter at the various stages of assessment and provision of services.

Culture is a central feature of a person's identity and that at the very least must be taken into consideration when working with service users from black and minority ethnic communities or when working with service users who are deaf.

Does the relative social exclusion that deaf people experience contribute to their mental health problems? This is reported as being a factor in the relationship between the psychological health of deaf people and their subsequent call upon mental health services. In other words being deaf can increase your vulnerability to mental health problems (Ridgeway, 1997). In Chapter 2 explanations are given of the cause and manifestation of mental health problems and in particular the role that stress plays in mental health.

Until recently mental health services seemed to be based around the assumptions that users were all from a hearing population that is predominantly white British. Both of these assumptions are well off the mark and need to be challenged and changed. To meet the NSF Standard One services need to be provided that are sensitised to the needs of different people. In reality the respect for the person's cultural identity is the predominant value that ought to underpin your practice.

CASE STUDY

Shaz is a deaf person who lives alone and, at the age of 32, has very few connections with the deaf community. She is a fluent user of British Sign Language but since her remand to prison on theft charges her health has suffered. Over the last ten years or so she has been treated for depression and has taken anti-depressants. The stress of being in prison has caused her more distress to the extent that she would like to see a social worker. However the prison service does not have a person who can sign and therefore they must seek outside specialist support. By chance the local community mental health team has a member of staff who can sign and she accompanies the social worker to the prison and carries out an assessment with the prison doctor.

This example shows how services can respond in an ideal way. However having a person who can effectively communicate in the same language as the service user is often a matter of luck and there is a need for more services of this nature. A deaf person who communicates through sign language is likely to find that being in an environment where fluent signers are is more conducive to their recovery than being in a hearing world. Of course once the specialist worker leaves the prison Shaz is left still having to cope with the traumas of prison, which is essentially a hearing world. This still leaves you having to explore with Shaz and the interpreter what specific needs she might have in respect to her deafness.

Learning disability and mental health

People who have a learning disability can experience a range of mental health problems just like the rest of us. However the presence of learning disability may prevent professionals and carers recognising the symptoms of mental health problems such as depression. It is important for carers and professionals to look beyond stereotypes and seek explanations for behaviour that has typically changed. Finding out what is wrong will call for quality communication and observation skills and working in a partnership with carers and service users. There are some informative guides published by the Royal College of Psychiatrists and the likes of MENCAP most of which you can download from their websites.

There are few research and evaluation studies in the field of learning disability and mental health – dual diagnosis is the technical term often used. This tends to maintain this important area as low priority yet Government policy expounded in the White Paper Valuing People urges people with learning difficulties to use mainstream NHS services. This of course includes mental health services. (Valuing People, March 2001)

The coexistence of mental health problems alongside learning disability may be one of the explanations of the existence of challenging behaviour. Such behaviour may not be a characteristic of learning disability but may be as a result of mental health problems. This is a theme that Moss picks up in his article in the *British Journal of Psychiatry*, which showed that there was 'some evidence for a statistical association between challenging behaviour and psychiatric disorder' (Moss, p.454). They concluded that depression was four times more prevalent in people with learning disability who exhibited challenging behaviour than for people with learning disability itself. This finding, although needing to be treated with some caution, is important as depression is so often overlooked in people with learning disability.

Working with service users who have this form of dual diagnosis often will mean mobilising community resources to provide support and connection with others in the community. This idea of connectedness is described by Peter Gilbert: 'Mental distress and mental illness is so often about a disconnection, false connections or an over concentration on one aspect of our lives'. (page 22). Like any other service user you as a social worker will want to access the whole person and how they draw support or otherwise from their families, carers and the community. Facilitating better connections within the community may be the most appropriate intervention that you can make.

Culturally competent practice: transforming social work

Cultural competence is a bringing together of some of the big ideas covered in this chapter. It is a combination of:

- awareness;

- knowledge of anti-oppressive practice;

- values based practice;

- interpersonal skills that will provide you with the basic building blocks of a practice that is appropriate; and

- sensitivity to working with service users who may not always be from your own culture.

A culturally competent service can be defined as one that is perceived by minority ethnic users

---

CASE STUDY

Christopher Clunis – inadequate care and treatment?

Christopher Clunis is a young Afro-Caribbean man who had a history of severe mental illness. He had been diagnosed as having paranoid schizophrenia when he lived in Jamaica. In December 1992 he attacked and killed Jonathon Zito who was completely unknown to him.

The subsequent inquiry has been widely reported and some of the findings reveal the perils of professional practice that is not culturally relevant.

15

The inquiry team concluded that:

The added factor of his blackness may have contributed to the diffident manner in which some professionals treated him and it may have caused them to defer against his best interests, to his own expressed wishes.
(Ritchie et al., 1994, p.4)

and

Young black males should not be type-cast as suffering from schizophrenia unless the clinical indications warrant it and clinicians and others who care for black mentally ill people should not be too ready to ascribe odd behaviour to the abuse of drugs.
(Ritchie et al., 1994, p.129)

---

as being appropriate to their cultural and religious beliefs and responsive to their needs.

This case study shows the extent to which stereotypical views can permeate professional practice and it highlights the dangers of seeing people only by the colour of their skin. Looking beyond this in a critical manner is the hallmark of good practice. At this point it is appropriate to examine the ways in which our practice can be transformed.

It should be clear that services need to become more relevant to the needs of black and minority ethnic groups and other minority groups such as people who are deaf. Service users frequently point out that the services that they are receiving show little understanding of their culture. But changing this is not a simple matter. You also need to recognise that this is a sensitive issue influenced by your own ethnicity and skin colour. Social workers who are skilled in anti-oppressive practice and using a values based practice approach are clearly further on than those who are not, but there is no room for complacency as many of the explanations of service variability show that racism permeates organisations.

It is questionable whether we can be competent in cultures that are not our own and in any case the range of diverse cultures in the UK makes competence in all cultures an unrealistic proposition. An alternative to understanding different cultures is to recruit more social workers and other professionals from these minority communities to ensure cultural congruence or, in other words, proportionate representation of professionals from all groups. However this can only be a limited strategy, for although positive action strategies when recruiting staff and adopting equal opportunities interview methods are vitally important, they are in themselves insufficient.

But what if you are a black social worker working with white service users or the other way around? What kind of approach can you adopt? To what extent do your stereotypes distort your assessment and decision-making processes? The National Institute for Mental Health England (NIMHE) has recommended that all staff working in this area receive compulsory training in cultural awareness to help eradicate racism and discrimination. Although there are many such courses around quite a few of these promote awareness rather than competency. Awareness is just one stage in developing culturally competent practice.

Components of culturally competent practice

The idea of being able to work with a diverse range of cultures is not entirely new but has gained momentum and acceptance of late. Walker (2003) uses the idea of cultural competence building on the work of Kim (1995), while Patel et al. in *Engaging and Changing* (2003) refer to practice as being 'culturally sensitive', whereas Fulford (in MHAC 10th Biennial 2001–2003) describes 'value based practice'. Some of the common themes are blended together into five components of culturally competent practice and each of these is explored below.

Capacity for your own cultural awareness
This should start with an honest understanding of your own culture and the impact that this has on your professional practice. You need to be aware of your own attitudes, values and beliefs before you can be aware of the attitudes and beliefs of others.

Capacity for awareness of other cultures
It is a widely held view that self-awareness is one of the core components of a practice that is culturally competent (O'Hagan, 2001; Poole, 1998, etc.) but after that it is necessary for you to develop your own capacity for understanding the other cultures and putting this understanding into practice. This requires you to make a realistic assessment of your knowledge and understanding of working with people and of their cultures.

Understanding of diversity and difference
Community engagement is currently being promoted as the main way that professionals can increase their understanding of specific needs of communities. Social workers should respect diversity and build upon people's strengths and the collective strengths of the communities. Effective work with and across cultures requires that you understand and value difference both at the individual and at the community level. This also means recognising and accepting your own personal and professional limitations.

Transferring skills from one service user culture to another
At the heart of much of professional practice is the idea that skills that are learned from work with one type of problem can be transferred to another. This means that the skills that you have in assessing white people who have depression can also be used when working with Asian people who have depression. But as we have seen earlier effective assessment requires you to understand the context in which the person is living. However social work skills such as empowering practice are key components of this transforming practice.

Being able to recognise the impact of structural racism and discrimination
Section 11 of the Health and Social Care Act 2001 places a duty on local health services to consult with services users and the public in the planning and development of services and this is an important step in the development of better and more appropriate services. Services are required to work *with* vulnerable groups and individuals at risk and to tackle social exclusion. This means that all providers of mental health services, including GPs and primary care workers, will be involved in some way or other in helping to deliver a service that is culturally appropriate and responsive to all groups in society.

Is it possible to achieve cultural competence?

The Government has established a five-year action plan called Delivering Race Equality in Mental Health Care, which is the main driver behind the attempt to achieve a culturally more responsive and capable workforce. As you can see from the list set out earlier this is a difficult task and not everyone thinks this will be achieved.

An interesting article in the *Guardian* should give cause for some healthy scepticism, a small extract of which follows:

> *Joanna Bennett, who leads research on workforce development at the Sainsbury Centre for Mental Health, has completed a review of race-related training and thinks that the picture is of 'a lot of fragmentation, different approaches and different models'. She says: 'There is no agreed definition of cultural competence and no evidence that it works in producing better services for black and minority ethnic users. We should be looking at structural processes and power relationships in the way services are delivered.'*

Bennett, a psychiatric nurse and former lecturer in mental health at Middlesex University, is the sister of David Bennett who died while in the care of mental health services. In evidence to the inquiry into his death, she warned against services focusing on 'cultural matching' in favour of staff spending more time talking to patients and thier families. Taking time to respect an individual, and ask what was troubling him and what he needed, was likely to be more effective than 'talking about culture, ethnicity and cultural competence' (*Guardian* Wednesday, 2006 April 12)

The significance of the above is that the inquiry into the death of Bennett, who had schizophrenia and who died during a restraint procedure at a medium secure unit, was that training for cultural competence was one of their high priority training recommendations. This followed the discovery during the inquiry that very little attempt had been made to understand let alone relate to the racial and cultural needs of David Bennett.

Achieving cultural competence may well require more than individuals alone can achieve although as Joanna Bennett points out getting the basis right will go a long way towards providing a more user focused service.

Promoting your own mental health

As you go through your course you are likely to be living a multitude of roles and having to meet numerous deadlines and expectations. These could include working to supplement your bursary or grant; balancing family life with college demands; worry about passing assignments and much more. Stress plays a big part in our own mental health and concern has risen in recent years over the increase in reported mental health problems for students in colleges and universities. In my experience social work students are no different from the majority of students studying on a variety of courses.

Students come to study at UK universities from all over the world and as a consequence the student community is as diverse as if not more so than the community at large. While many students can draw upon a range of personal resources, some are a long way from the support systems that have previously nurtured them. There are cultural differences which also may mean that they are unwilling to talk about personal issues with comparative strangers. It could also be that those who could offer help and may be concerned do not recognise the signs or mistakenly interpret these signs as cultural differences.

It might be that you recognise some of these elements in yourself and that you are reluctant to seek help, partly because of the possible impact on your studies. If this is getting to be a serious problem you should seek help as social work is a stressful career and you need early on to develop strategies that will enhance your own mental health for dealing with such stresses.

It is unlawful for universities to treat students with mental health problems that are substantial, adverse and long-term (more than 12 months) less favourably by excluding them temporarily or permanently if the reason is their mental health. Consequently a university should not exclude a student if their disruptive behaviour is primarily caused by mental health that falls into the realm of the Disability Discrimination Act 1995 (amended by the Special Educational Needs and Disability Act 2001).

Stress busting tip

The boxes technique

Think of a problem that you are currently dealing with (or have been recently) that has been causing you some concern, and how your mind goes over and over the problem. If that happens to you it can become stressful and unproductive. It can also prevent you from getting on with other things as your mind is focused on seemingly difficult problems. In time if this continues it can produce stress and perhaps sleepless nights. This is one technique for controlling and organising these problems that has been tried and tested by many students over the years.

1. Close your eyes and imagine that your mind is divided into a series of boxes and that each box has a lid.

2. Take each problem and place it into its own box.

3. Firmly place a lid on each box.

4. You now have your problems under control.

5. Only allow yourself to remove one lid at a time.

6. You can now focus all your attention on your released problem.

7. You may feel some of the lids on the other boxes starting to rise, if so be firm and replace them telling yourself that you will focus upon them at a later time. Persistent lid risers need a heavy weight to be placed upon them.

8. This technique really does work better with practice and students report that it is a good stress buster.

RESEARCH SUMMARY

The Mental Health Foundation commissioned research to overview current research and mental health initiatives related to student mental health. Among the findings was that clinical depression was reported in 12% of male students and 15% of females. This is an increase over the last time such estimates were made in 1987.

Student counsellors also reported an increase in the proportion of students with severe mental health problems or disorder. At the extreme end suicide among students has risen from 2.4 per 100,000 to 9.7. This is over the ten-year period 1983–1993/4.

(Fox, P. et al. in mentalhealth.org.uk/page.cfm?pagecode=PBUP0211)

CHAPTER SUMMARY

We have seen the impact that values and ethics have on mental health social work. These values are set down by the professional bodies and in the case of social work by the General Social Care Council.

Transforming social work in the twenty-first century requires workers to be able to recognise their own prejudices and biases and to move beyond these to develop a practice that is culturally competent, demonstrated by the worker's awareness of the service user's culture, including religion and traits. It also means looking after your own mental health and recognising that we all are susceptible to various mental health problems.

Transforming practice means also engaging in more than the rhetoric of anti-oppressive practice and value-based practice. It means demonstrating that these major ideas have influenced everyday mental health work. This means seeing the person not just as the mental health problem that they exhibit and not being influenced by stereotypes. Listening to what users have to say about their experiences is an important part of this process.

FURTHER READING

Department of Health (October 2003) *'Delivering Race Equality: A framework for action consultation document'*. London: DoH. A consultation document that sets out the 9 building blocks of improved practice for mental health services.

The Mental Health Act Code of Practice (DoH, 1999) gives specific practice guidelines when working with service users who are detained in psychiatric hospitals or units. It covers a range of activities including medication, other forms of treatment, control and restraint and what constitutes an emergency. This is essential reading for those who intend to practise in a mental health setting. NHS Trusts are advised to ensure that all staff undertake training in the meaning of the Code.

WEBSITES

The Internet Encyclopaedia of Philosophy has several pages concerned with the field of ethics and is a good place to visit for more information about 'normative principles in applied ethics'. www.utm.edu/research/iep/e/ethics.htm

Fox, P. et al. in mentalhealth.org.uk/page.cfm?pagecode=PBUP0211

RNID: fact sheet Introducing British Sign Language can be download free from www.ucl.ac.uk/library

Chapter 2

Social work practice and mental health

Introduction

> *The greatest happiness of the greatest number is the foundation of morals and legislation.*
> Jeremy Bentham. (1832)

This chapter introduces you to what is meant by mental illness and mental health. The dominant model of mental illness is medical, which is explored here. The importance of understanding not only what various diagnoses mean but also the implications of adopting the medical model is assessed. A contrasting perspective that incorporates social differences including gender, ethnicity, and age is also explored. Overlaid onto these differences are the social structural explanations that revolve around social exclusion and isolation, which will build on the foundations laid in Chapter 1.

This is not a medical text and you should use this text to guide your study rather than as a sole resource.

What is meant by mental illness and mental health?

The first point that needs to be made is that there are different terms currently used to describe the same thing. For example you will hear terms such as mental distress, mental illness, mental disorder, mental health problems, mental health challenges, all used by students and professionals.

In this book the following terms are used.

Mental disorder is a broad term that covers any significant departure from a state of 'normal' health and includes diseases and illness. These include severe forms like schizophrenia and manic depression. Mental disorder implies that a state of 'normality' once existed and therefore offers the chance to work with the person to restore them to that state, and is usually a temporary condition.

Mental health is a difficult term to be categorical about as it is far more than the absence of illness. I suggest that it is about achieving your potential as a human being. People can have mental health problems, which are 'problems of everyday life' which just have to be got on with.

Learning disability (formerly known as mental handicap and before that as mental deficiency). With learning disability the individual's rate of progress is slower than for most and treatment is not about a cure, as this is a long-term, permanent, condition, but about providing an environment in which the individual can achieve their potential.

RESEARCH STATISTICS

In 2000 the Office for National Statistics (ONS) carried out a survey of psychiatric morbidity of people aged 16 to 74 years living in private households in Great Britain, and it found that about one in six adults aged between 16 and 74 living in private households had a neurotic disorder, such as depression, anxiety or a phobia.

Lifetime experience of stressful life events: by type of event and gender, 2000: Social Trends 32

There are numerous perspectives about mental health and you need to get a good understanding of the various 'models' that are in current use. This means that you can evaluate one against the other and more importantly begin to put your practice in an appropriate framework. To help your understanding the **social model** and the **medical model** are described as two key perspectives that inform work with service users who have mental disorder.

First we should consider from where the general public gets information about mental disorder: by and large, through the media. The lay perspective, as it might be called, is important and few studies have examined how people conceptualise mental health. One of the few studies in this area showed that mental illness and mental health are seen by the public as being part of the same continuum and have negative connotations.

ACTIVITY **2.1**

Messages in the media

Think about the media coverage of mental illness and jot down the memorable words. Can you remember the last time that you read an article that was using positive adjectives or celebrating the success of people with mental health problems? What terms are used to portray mental health? Does this portrayal vary from media source to media source, from tabloid to serious newspapers?

You may well have written down terms like 'nutter' or 'looney' which are in common use and have negative connotations. These are some of the ways that behaviours can become associated with certain labels and consequently become self-fulfilling prophecies. What are your views about this? Is calling someone a 'nutter' just a piece of harmless fun or does it bring with it unwanted labels?

Words that are used by the media and in particular the tabloid press are often associated with violence and risk. Even though the risk of a stranger who is mentally ill killing you is very small, some of the press coverage suggests that it is a common occurrence.

Finally you might find it interesting to look at coverage in the press over the next few weeks and compare different newspapers and, if you have the time, think about how you would rewrite the headline or sub-heads.

Explaining mental health

It is easy to see that there are two perspectives about what causes mental health:

- that held by the medical practitioners which is essentially a biomedical or disease model;
- and that held by professionals like social workers which looks at social causation and/or labelling as explanations.

This separation into one or the other model is probably only useful in an academic or research sense as the medical perspective dominates and other perspectives need to at least take this perspective on board. This is now explored.

The medical model

This is a medical perspective that is adopted by doctors and psychiatrists and is sometimes called the 'disease model'. The acceptance of this model gives credence to the claim that organic or biomedical causes will eventually be found for all forms of mental disorder. Although the psychiatric model dominates discourse about mental disorder, this is as much by accident as it is by virtue of its conceptual strength. Andrew Scull, in his book *Museums of Madness* (1979), describes how a transformation occurred from people being seen as eccentrics, village fools or possessed by the demon when, around 150 years ago, the state took control and the medical profession was employed to treat and manage mental disorder.

In contemporary practice social workers work alongside other health professionals including psychiatrists to deliver mental health services. At some point you will be involved in an assessment of what the service users' needs are, which may necessitate a diagnosis.

Assessment

As a social worker you are most likely to be involved in this early stage of assessment and treatment of mental disorder. Campbell (1999) suggests that social workers can only become competent when, as a practitioner, they are able to synthesise interpersonal skills with theories and ideas about the causes of mental disorder. This is the case for all settings and aspects of the work. You may also be involved later in your career as an Approved Social Worker or similar with specific responsibilities under the legislation to assess a service user for whom compulsory admission to hospital may be the last resort. This is covered in the chapter on legal issues. An in-depth assessment would need to include some or all of the following:

- previous history of mental health problems or difficulties;
- service user self-assessment of their difficulties;
- cultural and religious aspects;
- employment status;
- relationship strengths and weaknesses;
- substance use or misuse including drug and alcohol use.

The importance of this approach is to identify what would be considered to be the most effective way of proceeding with the service user. The aim is to work in a manner that the service user would describe as culturally sensitive and which focuses upon the service user's strengths rather than deficits. Service users who have experienced mental health problems may have also experienced what works for them and your task may be one of mobilising resources to help them deal with their problems.

For those service users who are clearly presenting with behaviours that are likely to need more specialist services and possible medication, a referral to the GP and then to psychiatric services would be appropriate and even necessary.

Diagnosis

A diagnosis of mental disorder is always given by a doctor who is usually also a psychiatrist. It emerges out of considerable contact between the doctor and the service user. Assessment as described above is a process of collecting information that will assist in the making of a diagnosis. Conventionally the language of psychiatry replaces 'mental disorder' with the term 'mental illness' and 'service user' with 'patient'. Psychiatrists are trained to use a phenomenological approach, or in other words they try to establish a pattern of signs and symptoms. This helps to distinguish between people who are eccentric, unusual or who have only occasional symptoms from those whose symptoms indicate more severe disorder.

To avoid variation in assessment between doctors it is common to use one of a number of psychiatric assessment tools or interview schedules. These have all been standardised, a process by which the reliability of these tools is established. They help the psychiatrist to assess the presence of certain symptoms which act as signposts to effective diagnosis. The schedules include the **Present State Examination (PSE)**, which has 40 components to it, or the more commonly used **Beck Depression Inventory.**

The importance of a diagnosis is that it:

- acts as a pathway to more specialised care and treatment;
- is a process in which most patients have faith (sometimes in spite of the evidence);
- can mobilise support from other agencies such as housing and income benefit for those in need;
- should involve other professional views being sought, including those of social workers;
- should occur over a period of time and not be an assessment that is made over a few days, but rather weeks or even months.

However, service users seldom report the diagnostic process as being empowering and often complain that their views are seldom sought except as signposts to a diagnosis.

Classification of mental disorders

Classification is an important step in the diagnosis of mental disorder. Mental disorder is broken down into various classifications that represent groups or syndromes of symptoms or phenomena. Thus if a series of symptoms fits into a recognised pattern they can be classified as, for example, schizophrenia and a diagnosis made. A diagnosis is a short-hand version of what the psychiatrist believes to be wrong with the patient. Such classifications also enable treatment and outcomes to be better predicted. In the UK psychiatrists use one of two texts, either the **DSM-IV** (American Psychiatric Association's Diagnostic and Statistical Manual of Mental disorders) or the **ICD-10** (International Classification of Diseases Volume 10 (World Health Organisation, 1992)). Although as a social worker you will not be using these to diagnose it is worth familiarising yourself with some of the main features. This will help you to understand the basis of a diagnosis.

The nature of this process is rigorous and great efforts have been made to try to ensure their validity and reliability. For example the ICD, published in 1992, took nine years to prepare and was tested and included extensive field trials of the draft text in many countries

(Eldergill, 1997). Even so they have been the subject of dispute over the years (Menninger, 1963) and remember that a diagnosis is only as good as the information on which it is based. You might want to think about how much these diagnoses are affected by social factors, societal values and historical context.

Although as a social worker you are usually not directly involved with the determination of a diagnosis, you will need to share the ownership of it when working as part of a multi-disciplinary team. It is important that you have some understanding, at least of the main characteristics of the above and what the various treatment options are for each. You are also, more than most professionals, going to be involved in the complex interaction of the service user and their cultural and social background. For example with disorders like depression, which has a biological component to it, a combination of medication and social intervention is often the most effective treatment.

Treatment

There are different ways of treating users who have mental disorder. The effectiveness of such treatment depends upon the nature of the disorder and the skills of the people who are providing the treatment. These treatments are briefly discussed below. Every treatment option must have the risks weighed up alongside the possible benefits, for no treatment is without some cost and risk. Medical practitioners are trained first and foremost to do no harm to their patients. The dominant mode of treatment is medication but treatment also includes the following:

Psychosurgery
This is little used and then only for those with chronic conditions of obsessional and depressive disorders. It can only be given with the patient's informed consent, and Section 57 of the Mental Health Act (1983) applies to both informal and formal patients and provides additional safeguards. This is irreversible removal or destroying of brain tissue.

Electroconvulsive therapy (ECT)
ECT consists of administering an electric shock to patients who are sedated and is usually used when there has been an inadequate response to medication. It can be an effective treatment for depression, especially when this is accompanied by psychotic delusions. Patients are usually given a course of treatment of six to 12 applications.

Psychological
Psychological inputs are many and varied and include:

- behavioural therapy which is based on learning theory;
- cognitive therapy which focuses on incorrectly learned behaviours;
- counselling which also has numerous variants;
- psychotherapy which also includes many variants;
- family therapy.

Alternative medicine

As yet many of the 'alternative therapies', although popular with service users, are not 'proven' by research. They include hypnotherapy, dance, acupuncture and herbal remedies, and can have a role to play in combination with other modes of treatment. As interest continues some clinical trials have suggested that for moderate depression St John's Wort may be effective, and evidence suggests that exercise may also perform a valuable function.

Medication

Medication has become an important part of the treatment of mental disorder for many service users but it is not the only way of managing mental disorder. Medication works by either stopping the release of chemicals in the brain or by increasing the activity of certain parts of the brain. In the 1950s there was a 'pharmacological revolution' with the arrival of new forms of medical treatment including Chlorpromazine (Jones, 1993). This changed the lives of many patients with enduring mental illness in long-stay hospitals by giving them the opportunity to be treated in the community.

Today there is a 'new revolution' of 'atypical' anti-psychotic drugs, which have far fewer side effects than the previous ones and are also in many instances more effective. Some of the older medications caused amenorrhoea in women, which may have prevented long-term users from having children, whereas the main side effect of the new medication is significant weight gain.

Medication is divided into six types:

Type	Example	Typical use
Anti-psychotics	Chlorpromazine, Risperidone and in treatment-resistant conditions Clozapine	Schizophrenia
Anti-depressants	Prozac (fluoxetine)	Depression
Anti-manic	Lithium	Mania
Anti-epileptic	Carbamazepine	Epilepsy
Anxiolytics	Diazepam	Anxiety states
Hypnotics	Temezepam	Insomnia

RESEARCH STATISTICS

Over the past decade the number of prescription items for anti-depressant drugs dispensed in England has more than doubled, from 9 million items in 1991 to 24 million in 2001. The cost of anti-depressant drugs dispensed in the community in England was £342 million in 2001.

(1991 to 2001: Social Trends 33)

Understanding the major forms of mental disorder

The dilemma facing anyone who works with disturbed people is to be able to differentiate between 'normal' and 'abnormal' behaviour. The unusual behaviour or eccentricities of people are what make life so interesting and we should value such diversity. Clearly though there is a point beyond which the eccentric becomes markedly disordered and the person is in need of help. The main disorders that you will come across are described in the next part of this chapter.

Schizophrenia

Schizophrenia is a complex disorder with a number of variants, although the prognosis is well understood by specialists. It is a neuropsychiatric disorder where a number of factors may have impacted upon the central nervous system and which results in a cluster of symptoms that are classified as schizophrenia. It is commonly thought, incorrectly, by the general public to be associated with dangerousness and extreme madness and thus carries a stigma which other diagnoses do not (Eldergill, 1997).

Symptoms can include the following.

Hallucinations

These are problems to do with sensory perception, which are real for the person who experiences them. They include: auditory hallucinations (including hearing voices) and somatic hallucinations (the user believes that they are experiencing phenomena like electricity running through their body).

Delusions

These are beliefs which are considered bizarre, are clearly not supported by the available evidence yet are held in an unshakable manner by the person. Delusions can be part of systematic thought or appear to be completely random. These are usually culturally specific, hence in the UK some people are deluded into grandiose thinking, believing that they are related to the royal family or are relatives of the prime minister.

Interference with thought

Thought insertion is a form of delusion involving the belief that someone else's thoughts can be placed in the person's mind. This can also be perceived as a form of thought control where it is believed that someone outside is controlling your thoughts, or thought broadcast where you believe that your private thoughts are being broadcast to the general public.

Schizophrenia affects about 1% of the population. The onset is usually during adolescence or early adulthood but can occur later on in life. Before an accurate diagnosis is made the symptoms should have been noted over at least six months and must include at least one active psychotic phase. Early recognition and treatment significantly improves the overall prognosis for the user, consequently social workers should be aware of this and raise this diagnosis as a possibility rather than waiting to see. Early medication can alter the course of schizophrenia (Frangou and Bryne, 2000).

Features associated with schizophrenia

Episodes may consist of three phases in which 'normal functioning' is interrupted as follows:

1. **Pre-onset or prodromal phase** in which noticeable changes occur including social isolation, difficulty in functioning, odd behaviour, blunted affect, bizarre ideas, and lack of energy. Friends and relatives may describe the person's behaviour during this phase as 'he/she is not the same person as they were'.

2. **Onset or active phase** is where the behaviours and thoughts are acutely psychotic and often include delusions, which are false or irrational beliefs; hallucinations in which the most common is hearing voices; incoherence; belief that others can read your mind or hear your innermost thoughts and feelings of persecution. These need to be present for at least a week and can be the result of some stressful psychosocial event.

3. **Residual phase** is very similar to the pre-onset phase except that the person may experience negative affect and a flattening of emotions. They could still be hearing voices or other psychotic features but these are less strong.

Treatment and management

The usual treatment regime is a combination of medication and psychosocial interventions. While medication does not 'cure' it can dramatically correct serious and abnormal phenomena such as hallucinations or delusions.

The over-representation of young Afro-Caribbean males who are diagnosed as having schizophrenia is of major concern and points to the lack of culturally sensitive practice (see Chapter 1).

What is the social work role?

Social work intervention can include:

- education with the service user and their family;

- helping to arrange appropriate low stress accommodation;

- networking with the service user to provide community support;

- the use of behavioural techniques to modify behaviours;

- encouraging compliance with medication;

- acting as an advocate for the service user where appropriate.

What is the outlook or prognosis for people with schizophrenia?

About one-third of people who are diagnosed with schizophrenia will completely recover but for the remainder the outlook is one that will include at least one more episode, and for some schizophrenia will turn into a major challenge for them and their families or carers. The picture is much better than it was 20 years ago, in large part due to more effective interventions and the emergence of the newer anti-psychotic drugs that have fewer side effects than their predecessors.

(Chapter 6 has an illustrative example about schizophrenia).

Mood disorders: depression

Depression is a group of mental disorders that can affect many of us at some point in our lives. It can affect anyone, at any age, and is often overlooked among the very young and the elderly. Depression is a disorder characterised by mood change which explains why this disorder is termed a mood or affective disorder. There are different types of depression including manic depression, post-natal depression and clinical or major depression that affect about 3 – 4% of the population in any one year. More females are affected than males.

Depression is cateorised into three levels of severity: mild, moderate or severe. The ICD-10 is a good source for further information about these levels. However in essence the mild level allows users to receive treatment from their GPs and to continue with much of their lives; the moderate sees the user continuing their social, work or domestic lives with increased difficulty and with the severe it is unlikely that the user will be able to live a 'normal' life and suicide is a distinct risk.

Features associated with depression

Anyone can suffer from depression from time to time and it only becomes of clinical interest when the severity increases or the duration of the episode is longer than might be expected. Assessment is carried out using some psychiatric rating scales (Becks Depression Inventory).

Treatment and management

A range of treatments is possible depending upon the severity of the disorder. Among the treatments indicated are courses of anti-depressant medications, including the use of Prozac which interacts with the neuro-chemical pathways both in the brain and elsewhere in the body. The use of medication is often combined with psycho-social intervention to provide effective treatment. In severe depression it is important to take the risk of suicide seriously and to consult about risk with your medical colleagues. The user should always be asked about suicide, and where they exhibit plans for suicide or preoccupation with it then this should be seen as clear intent and action taken. (See Chapter 5 for an example on suicide.)

What is the social work role?

Social work interventions can include:

- identification of risk;

- management of risk;

- encouraging service users to take prescribed medication;

- individual counselling;

- cognitive behavioural therapy (CBT);

- referring for specialist psychotherapy;

- community networking.

Mood disorder: bipolar affective disorder (manic depression)

This is a disorder in which the person can feel intermittently depressed and occasionally elated. In the ICD mania and depression are cited as opposite ends of the same spectrum, hence the term bipolar. Mania is characterised by extreme elevation of mood and physical and mental energy and activity. It can exist in its own right (unipolar) but usually it is accompanied by at least one episode of depression. Because during mania the user believes that he/she is well, treatment is difficult and the social and financial consequences can be damaging as the person squanders their money or does other similar extravagances. Consequently hospital in-patient treatment may be required in order for the user's mood to return to normal.

The main medication is lithium although there are other medications available. This is a mood stabiliser that works by controlling the extent of racing thoughts rather than sedation, and although it takes a few days to work it does seem to prevent a swing into depression. It is particularly effective in the prevention of relapse among patients who have previously been diagnosed.

Dual diagnosis

The term dual diagnosis covers a spectrum of disorders that combine with mental disorder. While these can include mental disorder and learning disability they generally refer to mental disorder and substance abuse. This latter category has presented acute wards in hospitals with some of the most serious of challenges. In urban areas many of the patients admitted to hospital have experience of substance misuse, a habit which some try to continue while they are on the ward. The most common forms of misuse are drugs and alcohol.

The relationship between these conditions and the interactive effect are complex. These include:

- mental disorder that precipitated substance abuse;

- mental disorder which is worsened by the overlay of substance abuse;

- intoxication and/or substance abuse which results in psychological symptoms;

- withdrawal of substance abuse that results in psychiatric symptoms.

(Adapted from *Dual Diagnosis Good Practice Guide*, DoH, 2002)

Jacqui Smith, The Minister for Health, said in April 2002

> All too often people with 'dual diagnosis' – the twin problems of severe mental illness combined with drug and alcohol problems – have fallen between two stools, and been unable to find the help that they need from either mental health or substance misuse services.
> (Launch of the Acute In-Patient Care and Dual Diagnosis guidance, Jacqui Smith, 2002)

The National Office of Statistics demonstrated high levels of drug use in prisons, suggesting that 10% of remand prisoners had a moderate drug dependency, 40% had a severe dependency and among remand prisoners who were substance abusers over 75% had mental health problems (in *Dual Diagnosis Good Practice Guide*, 2002).

There is an increased risk of suicide for people with dual diagnosis and as substance misuse is becoming more common it should always be looked for in assessments. Treatment can involve motivational interviewing, assertive outreach, individual counselling and most importantly providing an integrated service. Associated with drug and alcohol abuse are increased physical health problems.

What is the social work role?
Social work interventions can include:

* identification of risk;

* management of risk;

* encouraging service users to take prescribed medication;

* cognitive behavioural therapy (CBT);

* community networking;

* liaison with other agencies and professionals.

Organic disorders

The organic disorders considered here are those associated with increasing age, most notably dementia. However don't forget that older people can also experience depression and other mental disorders in much the same way as their younger counterparts. The presence of depression in older people should be actively looked for and the person's presentation can mean that organic disorder is masked behind other mental disorders. For example approximately one person in five suffers from depression when they are over 60 and about one in ten actually develops depression after they have reached retirement age. There is a heightened risk of suicide among older people with depression.

Alzheimer's disease is a degenerative disease where the brain has been irreversibly damaged. Similar symptoms can also occur through excessive and prolonged consumption of alcohol or as a result of traumatic injury, a stroke or misuse of drugs. Sometimes the impairment can be acute and recovery is possible. In the case of Alzheimer's disease, which is considered to be a chronic condition, the brain progressively degenerates which results in impaired intellect, disorientation and eventually death.

Features associated with Alzheimer's
It is important to distinguish between the 'normal' effects of ageing and the development of a progressive disorder like Alzheimer's. We all suffer the loss of brain cells as we age but with this disorder cell loss is more rapid and profound than would be expected. The rate of degeneration does vary but it is usual for this to get more rapid as the disorder progresses.

Treatment and management
The early stages can be accompanied by depression, anxiety and severe sleep disturbance as the service user may have insight into the progressive nature of this disorder. Older people do better in familiar surroundings than in institutional care, but admission to residential care may be necessary where there is significant risk of self-neglect.

What is the social work role?

Social workers will work as part of a team that ideally will provide a system of care that encompasses the provision of support services of different kinds to the user and their carers, depending on their level of need. The social work role includes arranging welfare benefits, providing information and explanation of the user's situation to family, neighbours and others, arranging and financing social support systems and eventually specialist nursing care if necessary (Eldergill, 1997).

Critical psychiatry

While for the last fifty years the medical model has dominated the explanatory landscape there have been pockets of disaffection that have gained their followers. Among these several key names, themselves psychiatrists, are to be found including Thomas Szasz who in *The Myth of Mental Illness* was opposed to use of compulsion to treat people who in his view were struggling with problems of everyday life rather than some mental illness; Ronald Laing who saw the family and family power struggles accounting for much of what we call schizophrenia; and more recently a movement called 'Critical Psychiatry'. Psychiatrist Duncan Double is one of a small number of professionals who look beyond conventional explanations and treatment of people who have mental health problems.

Why is it that a movement called critical psychiatry can find favour? The answer lies in part in the general need by the public and professionals alike to examine alternatives to conventional treatments of a range of health problems. The increased use of supplements to assist diet, the use of acupuncture and homeopathy all stand testimony to the general dissatisfaction with the increased technical and scientific focus of medicine in general and by inference psychiatry. They do not absolutely reject the use of medication but rather put medication into a range of treatments rather than, as it sometimes is seen, as the only treatment.

The fundamental tenet of critical psychiatry is to challenge the evidence base and in so doing inevitably to look at the psycho-social aspects of the service users life. Phil Thomas, a Consultant Psychiatrist puts this over very succinctly on the critical psychiatry website www.critpsynet.freeuk.com/

> *Critical psychiatry is part academic, part practical. Theoretically it is influenced by critical philosophical and political theories, and it has three elements. It challenges the dominance of clinical neuroscience in psychiatry (but does not exclude it); it introduces a strong ethical perspective on psychiatric knowledge and practice; it politicises mental health issues. Critical psychiatry is deeply sceptical about the reductionist claims of neuroscience to explain psychosis and other forms of emotional distress. It follows that we are sceptical about the claims of the pharmaceutical industry for the role of psychotropic drugs in the 'treatment' of psychiatric conditions. Like other psychiatrists we use drugs, but we see them as having a minor role in the resolution of psychosis or depression. We attach greater importance to dealing with social factors, such as unemployment, bad housing, poverty, stigma and social isolation. Most people who use psychiatric services regard these factors as more important than drugs. We reject the medical model in psychiatry and prefer a social model, which we find more appropriate in a multi-cultural society characterised by deep inequalities.*

Double explains that the main aim of Critical Psychiatry is to develop a more open approach to psychiatry and that professionals like social workers need to remain sceptical about the claims that drug companies make for the efficacy of their products. This is not about ignoring the advances and assistance that medication has made but more about seeing this as only one component of the toolkit. (*Critical Psychiatry*: *Limits of Madness,* 2006).

To work in a truly empowering way can run counter to the imposition of a biomedical regime in which it is possible to see control and restraint as dominant features rather than enabling and understanding. It is important to understand the cultural context in which service users experience mental health problems and the role that poverty, poor housing and oppression play in someone's mental health. This is where the alternative explanation called the Social Model needs consideration.

The social model

The social model fits well with the general holistic approach of social work and is the underlying rationale for mental health social work although it is by no means as influential as the medical model. Nevertheless there are numerous examples of practice where the social model underpins effective practice (Ramon, 2001; Tew, 2002).

There are several different perspectives even within this model:

• social causation;

• labelling;

• critical theory;

• social constructivism; and

• social realism.

Whereas the conventional medical approach puts illness down to genetics, viruses or some other biomedical cause, the social model looks at social and environmental causes. The implications of the medical model are that illness *is* a matter of bad luck and one that needs an individual reaction, whereas the social model highlights the social causes and hence invites social reaction. This latter approach brings into play issues of power, oppression and social exclusion (Tew, 2002).

Social causation

Social causation is a particular perspective that helps us to understand the interaction between social disadvantage and mental disorder. A psychiatric diagnosis is largely accepted and the interest of the sociologist is in the effect that societal inequalities and social exclusion have had on the person's mental health. Other variables such as gender, ethnicity and class can be incorporated into this explanatory model.

The concentration of people who are diagnosed as having schizophrenia in inner city areas is an interesting example of this perspective. For although it is a 'fact' that the incidence of schizophrenia in inner city areas is much higher than in the suburbs and that schizophrenia is predominantly a lower class disorder, this is far from being a causal relationship.

ACTIVITY **2.2**

What factor do you think could explain the concentration of people with schizophrenia in inner city areas? Write down your ideas.

There are many possibilities but among those in the literature are:

- The drift theory, in which people who are long-term sufferers of schizophrenia migrate from rural areas into cities where they can blend in more easily and where services are more likely to be concentrated. People with schizophrenia from upper classes may find that the debilitating effect of this disorder results in them being unable to maintain their position in society and a downward drift into the lower classes occurs.

- Alternatively it could be that being in poverty in cities is harder and more alienating for people and that this could result in increased incidences of the disorder.

Labelling theory

Perhaps one of the most influential theories is labelling theory which describes a process by which '**primary deviance**' occurs, such as strange behaviour which continues to be interpreted as mental disorder or '**secondary deviance**'.

Primary deviance, or the initial concerning behaviour, may not always be recognised as a mental disorder as people often explain this initial deviance in terms of everyday behaviour. Thus the person with a drinking problem may be tolerated by their partner who has convinced himself or herself that their behaviour is just another way of letting off steam, or the more bizarre behaviour may be dismissed as humorous. Pilgrim and Rogers (1999) describe this as the 'clinical iceberg' (p.13) with many symptoms missed when doctors making diagnoses explain behaviours outside the norm for that person in terms of what should be rather than what is, happening.

Secondary deviance occurs when the diagnosis is made and the person takes on, or is seen to have taken on, the deviant role. In the same way that in primary deviance some behaviour gets interpreted as 'usual' then some of the deviant behaviour also is seen as what is typical of a mentally disordered person. The sociologist Erving Goffman (1961) describes this as the making of a psychiatric patient and writes about the role that the hospital plays as a total institution.

Psycho-social causes of mental disorder

The early part of this chapter concentrated on the medical model in which work with service users is focused upon trying to identify the cause of the mental disorder in order that we can intervene to restore better mental health. We then briefly looked at the social model and now need to see how these two models can be applied to everyday practice. Most professionals accept that the most likely cause of mental disorder is a complex interaction between a range of factors and that we need to find a way of encompassing biological, psychological and social factors that may be present. Newton (1988) is one of many academics who have constructed models that not only help us to see possible causes, but also to identify what might be done with the service user to improve their functioning.

A simplified version of these models is set out in Figure 2.1 and shows how factors can interact with each other to determine whether in any given circumstance a person will develop either good or poor mental health. These factors are:

- Predisposing or vulnerability factors including genetic components and previous family or personal history of mental health problems.

- Social causative factors including the importance of class, social exclusion and racism in reinforcing mental disorder.

- Psychological factors including loss, threats, highly critical relationships, resilience to adverse events and the extent of social support networks that precipitate or trigger the onset of disorder.

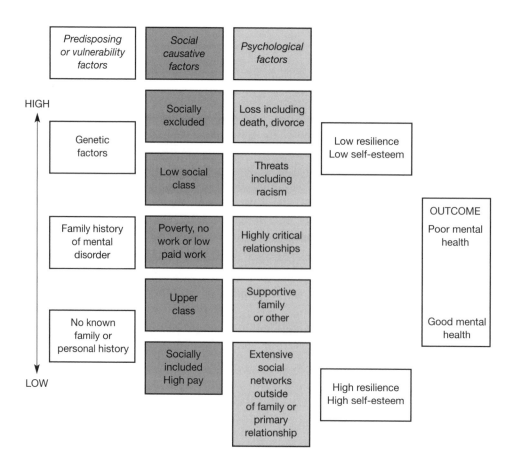

Figure 2.1: *Psycho-social model*

It is important that you realise that these models are an oversimplification of complex situations and that different authors use different terminology. Nevertheless they at least provide an indication of where people might be vulnerable and offer the possibility of intervention to help strengthen the weak areas.

This approach allows you to weigh up the factors and with the service user to work out what could be achieved to promote their mental good health. It also helps explain how people can face similar events but react differently. Thus although the service user may have a history of family mental health problems, they may be in a well-paid, satisfying job and with a network of social support. These factors could interact to provide protective rather than vulnerability factors. Of course the opposite might occur where no previous history of mental disorder is known but social exclusion and the resultant stress may increase the person's vulnerability to mental health problems.

Social work practice in a psycho-social context

The reality of intervening in people's lives is that you are working with something that is complex and multifaceted (O'Sullivan, 1999). At the centre of our work is helping service users to manage their lives in ways that are better for them and for their families and society. Any intervention carries with it a degree of uncertainty about the effect that this intervention might have on the service user.

The present drive to integrate services for people with mental disorder in theory opens up the opportunity to provide a seamless service. Social workers will work alongside health colleagues and it will be obvious to both just what they each bring to the situation. The need for quality evidence on which to support the specific intervention is long overdue and the establishment of centres for evidence-based practice (Huxley, 2002, p.198) suggests that social care is beginning to embrace the idea of measuring changes that have occurred as a result of their and others' interventions.

The Cochrane Centre provides systematic reviews of the effects of health care interventions and has a number of mental health groups in the collaboration, all of which can be accessed through their website: www.cochrane.org. The evidence that we have already shows that psycho-social intervention can have a powerful effect on rehabilitation; respite care to relieve the impact on carers can delay hospitalisation; family interventions can alleviate some of the negative aspects of living with someone who has mental disorder; intervention aimed at improving the living environment and creating or supporting social networks is effective; family work can be effective in reducing the emotionally charged and overly-critical family environments.

What works less well appears to be psychological debriefing after trauma, crisis intervention and case management (Huxley, 2002).

Examine Figure 2.1 and refer to either a case study that you know or one that is in this book. Lisa's story in Chapter 4 would work well for this activity.

Break down the case study into the factors that fit into this diagram and weight them according to your assessment of the likelihood of them increasing vulnerability or protecting against vulnerability to poor mental health.

You do not have enough detailed information to fully complete this task and that is perhaps the first important point to learn – analysis of causes is complex and requires careful collection of the 'evidence'.

The evidence that you have may well point to consideration of some of the factors such as does the service user belong to a black and minority ethnic group and if so is this likely to make them more vulnerable or less vulnerable? Similarly are they socially excluded? Is their financial situation stable?

If you work from right to left when looking at Figure 2.1 you should be able to get some idea of how various factors can interact to produce either a positive outcome or a negative one:

- **Predisposing or vulnerability factors** e.g. family with a history of mental disorder would make you more vulnerable to developing mental disorder.

- **Social causative factors** e.g. being unemployed or socially excluded (such as asylum seekers).

- **Psychological factors** e.g. no supportive relationships.

All of these factors could interact to produce low resilience, low self-esteem and therefore an increased likelihood of poor mental health.

You might want to think about what would have to change to increase resilience. A note of caution is needed, as it is unlikely that relationships between these factors would be simple or straightforward.

Stress is an intervening variable

Of course you probably realise that people experience similar events differently, the loss of job to one person could be a crushing blow that results in a vulnerability to depression yet to another it could be the very opportunity to go to college to get better qualified or to just take some time out. This will almost certainly be influenced by previous experience, family circumstances and financial position.

Epstein (1983) suggests that it is possible to learn better ways of coping with stress while writers like Cochrane (1983) point to the role that stress plays in pushing people either towards positive mental health or in the other direction. It is not just the experience of losing your job but the way in which this impacts upon you and, importantly, how you perceive the event. This approach does open up the prospect of working with the service user to recognise what makes them overstressed and to identify better ways to manage their stress. It is clearly not possible to reduce all the adverse events that affect a person's life but it is possible to get better at managing the situations that might cause them and their reactions to them.

EXAMPLE

Social workers working with families and young people who are on the road to recovery from an eating disorder can do work on some of the factors that cause the service user to feel under pressure about their eating habits, Among these short-term techniques are included:

- *not asking about what person has eaten;*

- *avoiding making comments about the food;*

- *not making comments about shape or size;*

- *not telling them that they look good or healthy;*

- *not making any comments about their weight.*

This puts the consideration of weight and size into the professional domain and removes everyday comments from family members that may be considered stressful.

Promoting mental well-being: a political approach

Newton provides information about what is needed to provide the necessary conditions to prevent mental disorder. Two possible approaches to prevention are either to work to reduce the vulnerability factors, or helping people to develop more positive responses and increased resilience to withstand stressful situations. It is a political approach as many of the social factors include the effects of social exclusion, racism and poverty.

Work that falls into the category of reducing vulnerability would include social workers being placed in schools and projects with specific funding, such as Sure Start. In both instances the work can be focused upon the young person and their families. Some of the work compensates for social disadvantage and could have a positive impact on mental health.

Promoting positive mental health: saving lives

Our Healthier Nation (1999) was a direct attempt by government to create a healthier nation by reducing the incidence of mental disorder. In 2003 the then Minister for Health Jacqui Smith launched England's first ever national suicide prevention strategy. It is hoped that by identifying key factors that are associated with suicide such deaths could be significantly reduced.

ACTIVITY **2.4**

Go back to Figure 2.1 and think where would be the best focus for a suicide prevention strategy. What factor would make people more vulnerable to suicide thoughts? Jot down your ideas.

39

You probably came up with most of the factors that are identified in the policy document. These would include people who are:

- in low paid, unskilled work;

- unemployed;

- breaking up from their relationship;

- socially isolated;

- misusing drugs or alcohol.

Having an impact in all these areas would help and we do not actually know which one would make the biggest difference. This requires a mixture of social policy and community initiatives.

Equally, working with service users who are depressed to improve their social networks would help, and so would encouraging service users to continue taking their medication.

Despite the methodological problems the government has moved forward with its intentions to affect the number of suicides with year-on-year reductions set as targets. Progress is being made but even so over 1,300 young adult men take their own lives each year in England, a number which has now overtaken road deaths as the biggest killer of young men in this age category (Brock and Griffiths, 2003). Overall over 4,500 people take their own lives each year. Some of the actions that have been taken include:

- Reducing the pack sizes of aspirin and paracetamol in an attempt to make it more difficult for people to purchase large quantities of these tablets.

- Improving the risk assessment on inpatient wards where acute patients are liable to be detained.

- Establishing a research forum to improve the quality of the information that is available to professionals to ensure that professional practice is evidence based.

- Working more closely with service user groups.

- Setting up a number of pilot projects to target key at-risk groups such as young men.

With the last two actions social workers will be among the key professionals who will help to put these initiatives into operation.

It is too early to comment authoritatively about the effectiveness of this plan and authoritative evaluations are needed.

C H A P T E R   S U M M A R Y

This chapter has introduced you to the two main theoretical approaches to understanding mental health. As required by the subject benchmark you should have developed your knowledge of the critical and research-based explanations that contribute to the knowledge base of social work, including the application to practice. As a social worker you need to have at least a basic understanding of the medical model and the major mental illnesses that can affect service users. This will enable you to have more meaningful dialogue with medical colleagues and to work in an informed way with service users.

Detail has been provided about mental disorder, intervention and treatment. Included in this has been a description of the main types of medication that are currently in use, and all this should help you to feel more confident and knowledgeable about mental health. The role of social workers in working with people who have mental disorder or mental health problems has been outlined and the provision of a schematic outline of psychosocial factors will help you to see where the best intervention ought to be made. As this model underpins most of social work practice when working with people who have mental health problems, it will be referred to over the next chapters.

In-depth case studies are provided in later chapters that build up your specific knowledge of depression, schizophrenia and eating disorders.

Stress busting tip

Preventing stress and promoting positive mental health by developing an effective support system

As you have seen in this chapter stress can play a large part in our mental health and can trigger mental health problems and disorder. Having a support system that provides support for you can help you and others to deal effectively and more healthily with stress. This support can be informal or formal, the key is what works for you. What does help is being able to talk things through with someone who helps you to see the positive side of things and can help you to construct solutions rather than dwelling upon the problems. This should help you to move into a 'glass half full' perspective rather than a 'glass half empty' one.

Consider your own support systems. If possible find a friend and go through this list recording your answers. The content of the discussion is confidential to you and you should only discuss what you feel comfortable with.

Support network

Do you currently have:

1. Someone on whom you can rely in a crisis?

2. Someone who makes you feel good about yourself?

3. Someone you can be totally yourself with?

4. Someone who will tell you, honestly, how well or badly you are doing?

5. Someone you can talk to if you are worried?

6. Someone who really makes you stop and think about what you are doing?

7. Someone who is lively to be with?

8. Someone who introduces you to new ideas, new interests, new people?

Of course to find all these 'ideal type' attributes in one person would be truly special and even if you did find such a person, putting all of this on them might be too much and put a strain on relationships. There are also key times when we may need extra support and have to either seek professional help or develop a new network.

If you have been able to reflect on this list you may now want to reflect a little more.

Is your support coming from one person? Is this from home or student life? Do you need a better balance between these two? What gaps have you got in your support network? What are you going to do about these gaps? If you have more gaps than you would like, work out how to alter this – you may want to find someone who can help you, perhaps a student counsellor.

FURTHER READING

Anselm Eldergill's, (1998) seminal work *Mental Health Review Tribunals: Law and practice* is a classic in its own right and a surprisingly rich source for anyone who wants to read in depth on the origins, causes and treatment of mental disorder. In the 300 pages devoted to these topics he shows a remarkable grasp of detail and an enviable ability to explain these to non-medics. His work has greatly influenced the content of this chapter.

D Pilgrim and A Rogers', (1999) *A Sociology of Mental Health and Illness* (2nd ed) is a best-selling text and one of a number of texts that illustrate the key perspectives on mental health. It has good chapters on social class inequalities and mental health, gender, race and ethnicity and age, all of which make for interesting and relevant reading.

WEBSITES

Social Trends can be downloaded free from www.statistics.gov.uk

Chapter 3
The legal and political context

Knowledge of legal rules and their application to practice are features in the social work subject benchmark statements which universities must meet and such knowledge and application inform the National Occupational Standards.

This chapter will help you to begin to meet the following National Occupational Standards.

Key Role 1: Prepare for and work with individuals, families, carers, groups and communities to assess their needs and circumstances

- Assess needs and options to recommend a course of action.

Key Role 2: Plan, carry out, review and evaluate social work practice, with individuals, families, carers, groups and communities and other professionals

- Interact with individuals, families, carers, groups and communities to achieve change and development and to improve life opportunities.
- Address behaviour which presents a risk to individuals, families, carers, groups and communities.

Key Role 6: Demonstrate professional competence in social work practice

- Research, analyse, evaluate and use current knowledge of best social work practice.
- Work within agreed standards of social work practice and ensure own professional development.

It will also introduce you to the following academic standards as set out in the social work subject benchmark statement, which includes:

4.3 Defining principles

There are competing views in society at large of the nature of social work and its place and purpose. Social work practice and education inevitably reflect these differing perspectives on the role of social work in relation to social justice, social care and social order.

5.1.1 Social work services, service users and carers

- The nature and validity of different definitions of, and explanations for, the characteristics and circumstances of service users and the services required by them, drawing on knowledge from research, practice experience, and from service users and carers.

5.1.2 The service delivery context

- The significance of legislative and legal frameworks and service delivery standards (including the nature of legal authority, the application of legislation in practice, statutory accountability and tensions between statute, policy and practice).
- The complex relationships between public, social and political philosophies, policies and priorities and the organisation and practice of social work, including the contested nature of these.

5.1.3 Values and ethics

- The nature, historical evolution and application of social work values.
- The moral concepts of rights, responsibility, freedom, authority and power inherent in the practice of social workers as moral and statutory agents the complex relationships between justice, care and control in social welfare.
- The practical and ethical implications of these, including roles as statutory agents and in upholding the law in respect of discrimination.

5.2 Subject-specific skills and other skills

As an applied subject at honours degree level, social work necessarily involves the development of skills that may be of value in many situations (for example, analytical thinking, building relationships, working as a member of an organisation, intervention, evaluation and reflection). Some of these skills are specific to social work but many are also widely transferable. What helps to define the specific nature of these skills in a social work context are:

- The context in which they are applied and assessed (e.g., communication skills in practice with people with sensory impairments or assessment skills in an interprofessional setting).
- The relative weighting given to such skills within social work practice (e.g., the central importance of problem-solving skills within complex human situations).

Introduction: the need for legislation?

The end of law is, not to abolish or restrain, but to preserve and enlarge freedom.
(John Locke, 1690)

People who have mental health problems from time to time become vulnerable and a small but significant number may need treatment and care, even if this is against their wishes at the time. Such is the nature of mental disorder. Compulsory admission to hospital is just one part of the legislative framework but is so significant because of the potential infringement of the person's human rights. The implication for us as social workers is clear: if we are to be competent practitioners in mental health then we need to understand the relationship between the law and our practice and how to respond in different situations and to be able to work across organisations.

Just how much mental health law should be known by non-specialists is open to dispute but what is certain is that each and every one of us will work with people who have mental health problems and on occasion we will work with people who may be subject to some of the many parts of mental health legislation. Therefore it is important that all social workers, social care workers and nurses are familiar with the basic provisions of the law relating to mental health and some of the underlying tensions that exist in its execution including the importance of ethics and values.

This chapter will provide essential basic information about two important pieces of legislation, both amended in 2007 with most provisions being in place by late 2008. Unlike previous chapters, there is only one case study, albeit a long one, for you to work through instead of smaller activities. Bear in mind that all law is experimental and subject to change and that there is no substitute for reading the actual statutes, codes of practice and regulations. Keeping up to date is essential not only to maintain your registration but also to ensure that you can engage with service users, carers and other professions in a manner which exudes confidence that is founded on accurate information.

A very short history of mental health law

'Mad' people only became the concern of the public from about the middle of the eighteenth century, a point in history that coincides with the impact of modernism with the increased focus upon rationality and reason as characteristics of man (Shaw, 2007). Prior to this if you had mental health problems you were more likely be kept within the family or to become one of the poor souls in the local workhouse. The perception that madness was the loss of reason and rationality resulted in a range of responses from locking people up to providing care and treatment.

During the early nineteenth century, county asylums developed with the aim of providing refuge and tranquillity during which time the resident would be able to recover their reason and rationality and be treated with respect. It was the job of magistrates to order admissions to such hospitals. At the same time private mad-houses flourished and soon thereafter concerns of abuse and ill treatment were voiced, which resulted in the Madhouse Act of 1828. The continuing calls for regulation led to the 1845 Lunatics Act being passed by Parliament. At this time treatment was limited and the medical profession had little involvement and it was a while before madness became inextricably linked with the medical profession and the law. Locking people away in an asylum with various restraints became a familiar theme with the likes of Charles Dickens and other writers.

 The growth in Europe of a treatment based upon the calm care for patients emerged in England at the York Retreat and was largely due to the influence of Tuke (1813) and earlier Pinel in France (1774). Through this approach it was expected that restraint could be replaced by helping people to regain their self-control of their madness.

Although the early reformers were enlightened social thinkers, it wasn't too long before the focus on 'moral treatment' once again gave way to a greater emphasis on the control of inmates' madness and the restriction of their liberty. The focus had again shifted to the need to 'protect the public' and in the 1890 Lunacy Act we witness the dominance of the legal profession and legal procedures over social reform and treatment.

This tension between treatment of the individual and the protection of the public can be seen to influence the development of our responses to mental health problems. First we move one way and then to another. In 1930 the Mental Treatment Act shifted the focus from custody and protection once again towards treatment and prevention. This reform was, according to some writers, a direct response to the emergence of treatments like insulin-coma therapy, electro-convulsive therapy and brain surgery (Shaw, 2007). This Act also introduced the first ideas about treating people in the community although it was many years before a significant move to the community actually occurred. Kathleen Jones, the first woman professor of social policy to be made a member of the Royal College of Psychiatry, describes the 1950s as a time when the three revolutions occurred (Jones, 1975). The first of these was the sudden advance in major medication and the arrival of antipsychotics like chlorpromazine, which enabled the more florid symptoms in patients to be subdued; the second was the modernisation of hospitals and the increased range of facilities that were on offer; and the third revolution was the major legal reforms brought about in the 1959 Mental Health Act, principles of which still underpin modern-day legislation.

The move away from large asylums (psychiatric hospitals, as they were becoming known as) began to take hold in the late 1950s when two powerful forces happened to coincide. The first of these was largely a response to scandals about hospital care and a reaction to the reality that many patients on long-stay wards had become institutionalised and therefore unlikely ever to be able to leave the regime of institutional care. The second was the view, false as it proved to be, that care in the community would in fact be cheaper than keeping patients warehoused in expensive hospitals. Such tensions are still present today.

The 1983 MHA was built upon the basic principles of the 1959 Act and even though the 2007 Act has made some significant changes the basic law remains. The 1983 Act saw the introduction of the approved social worker, who was a more skilled replacement for the 1959 mental welfare officer. It also introduced a strong legal framework and procedures in which any decision to admit someone to hospital had to be made. The influence of an American lawyer Larry Gostin, sometimes called the 'father of the Act', was evident with legalism embodied in this statute.

Calls for a more patient-centred and more imaginative legal framework gathered momentum from the late 1990s. At the same time public coverage of murders by ex-patients of mental hospitals meant that the government was anxious to put right as they saw it deficiencies in community care. One such murder was that by Christopher Clunis, who in 1992 stabbed Jonathan Zito, a complete stranger, in the eye, killing him. Jonathan, who had just arrived in the UK from Italy and was recently married, was waiting for an underground train with his brother at the time. Clunis was a well-known psychiatric patient, recently discharged, with a diagnosis of paranoid schizophrenia and a history of violence and non-compliance with treatment programmes. This resulted in calls for tighter surveillance and better resources for patients like Clunis to both protect them but also to protect the 'innocent' public.

Once again we can see tensions between the government's increased preoccupation with risk and control and the conforming to human rights legislation.

It was this preoccupation with managing risk and the new need to be compliant with human rights legislation, both hallmarks of a modernist agenda, that was to bring about confrontations between bodies like the Royal College of Psychiatry, the Mental Health Alliance and others to oppose many of the proposals by the government. The tension between personal freedom and protection of the general public had risen to the surface and was eventually to prevent the introduction of an entirely new law. The original reform process was initiated by the government in 1998, with a call for the most wide-ranging reform of mental health legislation since the 1950s. In 2002 and 2004, the government published proposals for new mental health legislation in England and Wales in the form of draft Mental Health Bills. However, faced with considerable opposition the proposals were abandoned in March 2006. In its place the government drafted a more streamlined proposal to amend the 1983 Act. The Bill was eventually introduced on 16 November 2006 and received Royal Assent on 19 July 2007. It reflects government concerns about managing risks and amends the Mental Capacity Act by introducing deprivation of liberty safeguards (DoLS), which should comply with human rights legislation.

The large majority of people who have mental health problems do not need specialist treatment and even within this group there are many who can be treated in the community. Where hospital admission is indicated and they have capacity and the person is unwilling to go in, it must be that they have a mental disorder within the meaning of the Act that is of a nature or a degree that warrants detention and that this detention is necessary. The majority of admissions are through a civil process that does not involve courts but there are occasions when mentally disordered offenders may be detained in a psychiatric hospital or be transferred from prison to such a hospital.

However, not everyone is satisfied that the confrontational process that the government engaged with over reform has produced legislation that is in any way ground-breaking. In a press release the Mental Health Alliance claimed:

> We now have a Bill that for the first time gives people a right to an advocate when they are detained and that protects children from being put on adult wards inappropriately. We also have new safeguards over the use of electro-convulsive therapy, for people detained under the Mental Capacity Act, and for the renewal of detention. These are hard-won improvements that are a credit to the persistence of activists from across the country.
>
> But our members will be disappointed today that the Government has rejected changes to many other aspects of the Bill. It has failed to heed the evidence about the risks of significant over-use of community treatment orders and the excessive powers the Bill gives to clinicians. And it treats people with mental health problems as second class citizens by allowing treatment to be imposed on those who are able to make rational decisions for themselves.
>
> (Mental Health Alliance, July 2007 press release)

The legislation

The government changed the law about mental health after a lengthy period of debate and confrontation between a wide variety of interested parties and most of these provisions come into being by October 2008. This new law is called the Mental Health Act 2007 and amends the Mental Health Act 1983. This means that although the basic legislation remains the Mental Health Act 1983 we need to be familiar with the main provisions and amendments of this new legislation. This also introduces the deprivation of liberty safeguards (DoLS) – implementation planned for April 2009 – as an amendment to the Mental Capacity Act 2005. In a similar vein, the Domestic Violence, Crime and Victims Act 2004 is amended to increase the rights of the victims of crimes carried out by mentally disordered offenders.

There will be a new Mental Health Act Code of Practice to accompany the Mental Health Act 2007. As before, although the MHA Code is not law, you must have regard to what it says, and if not you must be able to justify why you have not heeded its guidance. This chapter will examine some of the changes that make up the Mental Health Act 2007 and the guidance contained within the new Code of Practice.

The amendments to the legislation are carried out through a process of commencement orders that are made under the Mental Health Act 2007 and bring into force on certain dates the provisions of the amendment act for example substituting references to 'an approved social worker' for those to 'an approved mental health professional'.

The Mental Capacity Act 2005 and the Mental Health Act 2007

Although every attempt has been made to guarantee accuracy, there is no substitute for going back to first principles and reading the Mental Health Act, the Mental Capacity Act and their associated Codes of Practice. The term 'patient' is used in the legislation, as is the male pronoun, and to avoid confusion these terms are used in this chapter.

Main purpose

The main reason for this new legislation is to provide a process by which a person with a mental disorder can be detained for treatment with or without his or her consent. It also provides legal processes that must be followed in order to safeguard the rights of the patient. The Department of Health overview states:

> *The main purpose of the legislation is to ensure that people with serious mental disorders which threaten their health or safety of the safety of the public can be treated irrespective of their consent where it is necessary to prevent them from harming themselves or others.*
> (Department of Health guidance, 2007)

There are three ways in which a person may be admitted to a psychiatric hospital.

- Informally, which is often referred to as voluntary admissions which is covered by s.131.

- Under the Deprivation of Liberty procedures in the amended Mental Capacity Act 2005.

- Compulsory detention under part 2 or part 3 of the MHA 1983.

Informal admission

If a person is capable of deciding whether to be admitted to hospital, he may be admitted with his consent. If he is refusing to consent he may not be admitted as an informal patient and the only option will be to detain him under the MHA 1983. An incapable patient may be admitted informally, but only if his care does not amount to a deprivation of liberty. An incapable patient may only be deprived of their liberty in accordance with new legal safeguards, referred to as deprivation of liberty safeguards (DoLS).

If a person with mental disorder needs to be admitted to hospital in the interests of his health or safety or for the protection of others and resists admission, then it is likely that they will be detained under the MHA 1983. If, however, he lacks capacity but is otherwise compliant with his treatment, his care will most likely be given under the MCA 2005.

There are circumstances where even if the patient agrees to go into hospital but is considered to be a danger to themselves or to others, that compulsory detention may be justified.

Mental Capacity Act 2005 (as amended)

Until recently, informal admission was used not just for those who agreed to admission but also for incapable patients who were not actively resisting or protesting against their admission. Such a course was felt to be lawful under the common-law doctrine of necessity.

This changed with *HL v United Kingdom*, when the European Court of Human Rights (ECHR) noted that where a person is subject to such a degree of control over his basic human needs that he is deprived of his liberty, this will only be lawful if there is an adequate 'procedure prescribed by law'. The conclusion they reached was that in the case of incapable patients Informal Admission under s.131 was not such a procedure. HL was an autistic man who could not speak and it was clear that although he was held as an informal patient, if he decided to leave he would have been prevented from doing so. He was at the time admitted to a hospital run by the Bournewood Trust and because of the nature of his care was, the ECHR found, deprived of his liberty. This situation is unlawful because the common law of necessity is too vague and has too few effective safeguards to comply with Articles 5(1) and 5(4) of the ECHR. Thus HL was *de facto* detained and the DoLS represent the government's attempt to remedy the problem that Bournewood case highlighted.

Hence, the MCA applies to people who are admitted to a NHS hospital, an independent hospital or another residential facility who lack the capacity to consent to their admission but who are nonetheless, deprived of liberty (Fennell, 2007).

For any such deprivation of liberty to be lawful, it will have to have been authorised under the formal procedures set out in the DoLS. There are five points that you should understand.

- Always assume that someone has capacity.

- Understand what is meant by capacity.

- Treat everyone equally.

- Support the person to make their own decision.

- Assess capacity using a two-stage test:
  - Does the person have an impairment of the mind or brain or is there some sort of disturbance affecting the way that their mind or brain works?
  - If so, does that impairment or disturbance mean that the person is unable to make the decision in question at the time that it needs to be made?

What is capacity?

Mental capacity is the ability to make a decision which can affect everyday decisions, like when to get up, what to wear and when it is necessary to go to the doctor's. It also refers to making decisions that could have legal consequences either for themselves or others, like making a will or agreeing to have medical treatment.

Section 2 of the MCA 2005 states that a person lacks capacity if they are unable to make a decision, and sets out the following as a test. Is the person able to do the following?

- Understand the information that is needed to be able to make a decision.

- Retain the information.

- Use that information when trying to decide what to do.

- Communicate the decision (called the 'statutory test').

What authority is responsible?

Two new legal entities have been introduced.

Managing Authorities who provide care and who need authorisation to provide care that amounts to detention. In the case of a private hospital or care home, it is the 'person registered' who is the managing authority, whereas for the NHS, it is the NHS body responsible for the management of the hospital.

Supervisory bodies who must organise assessment to determine, among other things, if detention is in the best interests of the patient and issue authorisations if appropriate. Supervisory bodies for a patient in a hospital will usually be the primary care trust (PCT) that commissions the relevant treatment; where a care home is concerned it will be the local authority.

'Bournewood' deprivation of liberty safeguards (DoLS)

- Section 50 of the MHA has amended the MCA 2005 to provide safeguards for those incapable people over 18 years of age that are deprived of liberty. The government hopes this will meet the requirements of the ECHR although we will have to wait until it is tested in the courts.

If in the case of a particular adult, no authorisation has been obtained under the DoLS, a deprivation of liberty will only be lawful if :

- It is the subject of an order made by the court of protection under s.16(2) of the MCA; or

- an application has been made to the court and, in the meantime, it is necessary to save the person's life or prevent serious deterioration in his condition.

Best interests

It is a fundamental principle that any act or decision made for or on behalf of a person who lacks capacity is made in their best interests. This means that account will have been taken of the medical and non-medical effects and the overall welfare interests of the patient and the possible impact on their families. Section 4 of the MCA sets out the approach that must be used and just what must be taken into account when a best-interest assessment must be carried out.

There will be best interest assessors (BIA) who will be trained by the providers of AMHP training, and there will be mental health assessors (MHA) who will undertake training provided by the Royal College of Psychiatrists.

Advance directions

Under the MCA ss.24–26, an adult while capable, may refuse medical treatment that would otherwise be provided to him in the future, when he had become incapable. This is now known as an advance direction (it was previously known as either an advance directive or a living will). If when the person has become incapable, the treatment in question would sustain his life, his refusal will only be binding if it is in writing and complies with other MCA formalities. In this way a person might refuse medical treatment that would have been given compulsorily under the MHA 1983. However, it might have some use in mental health care – for example, to prevent mental treatment being given to an informal, incapable patient (whose care would otherwise be given to him under the MCA) or in the case of a detained patient to prevent treatment being given to him for something other than mental disorder).

Court of Protection

Where an adult lacks capacity in relation to his health care or social care or his property or financial affairs, it is possible that the Court of Protection could make an order in that regard or appoint a deputy to makes decisions on the person's behalf. The Court can only make an order to deprive an incapable person of their liberty if the requirements of the MCA 2005 Sch. 1 are met.

Independent mental capacity advocates (IMCAs)

The Mental Capacity Act (MCA) introduced the role of independent mental capacity advocates (IMCAs) on 1 April 2007 (October for Wales) and the statutory requirement to provide a specialist advocacy service for a specified group. This is a new and important safeguard for people who lack capacity and who have no one, other than paid staff, to support them. This it is estimated will have an annual cost of £6.5 million for England (Curran and Grimshaw, 2007).

The word 'advocate' originates from the Latin *advocatus*, meaning legal witness of counsellor. This is different from the role that IMCAs will play as they are described as *non-instructed advocacy*, as they are not taking instructions from the patient who benefits from their service. This is logical as the patient is deemed not to have capacity and therefore would find it difficult to instruct an advocate.

Criteria for IMCAs
Where a person who lacks capacity and is without friends or relatives with whom to consult, decision-makers in local authorities, NHS trusts and care homes have a duty to consult with an IMCA. A person may be referred to the IMCA service if:

- they lack the capacity to make a decision;
- this decision involves changes to their long-term accommodation, e.g. under after-care, s.117 1983 MHA;
- they need serious medical treatment, e.g. surgery;
- they are subject to a care review and no one else is available to be consulted;
- they are in need of protection as a vulnerable adult whether or not family, friends or others are involved.

In practice IMCA clients will include those who are unconscious, have dementia, serious physical and or mental health problems as well as end-of-life decisions.

Principles underlying the MHA 1983 (and the MHA 2007 Amendment Act)

Unlike Scottish Mental Health legislation, which includes overt principles, the law for England does not and it is to the Code of Practice that we must look to find a statement of guiding principles, and these are set out below. These are essentially those that underpinned the 1959 MHA.

Purpose

Decisions under the Act should be taken with a view to minimising the harm done by mental disorder, by maximising the safety and well-being (mental and physical) of patients and protecting them from harm.

Least restrictive alternative

Any intervention without the patient's consent must attempt to minimise the restrictions on the patient's liberty having regard to the purpose for which they are imposed.

Respect

Diversity should be recognised and all workers should be aware of different cultures and how some behaviour may be misconstrued as mental disorder. The patient's wishes and feelings should be respected at all times and care should be taken to ensure that there is no unlawful discrimination.

Participation

Patients should be involved, as far as is practicable in the circumstances, in planning their own care and treatment to ensure that it is as effective and appropriate as possible. The involvement of carers, family members and others who have an interest in the patient's welfare must be encouraged (unless there are particular reasons to the contrary).

Resources

Decision-makers must seek to use whatever resources are available in an efficient, effective and equitable way. Decision-makers must take into account other people's perspectives on what is required.

The structure of the MHA 1983

The Act has ten parts and within these a variety of sections. Throughout this chapter you will see references to different parts of the Act. For example, you may find reference to Part 2 patients, who are people who have been made subject to some form of compulsory intervention under the Act in their own interests or to protect other people, without the involvement of the courts. They are also often known as 'civil patients'. Part 3 patients are those who have been made subject to a compulsory intervention under the Act by the courts, or who have been transferred to hospital from prison or another type of custody.

KEY FACTS

- *The number of detentions under the Act rose to 48,000 in 2006–07 from 47,400 in 2005–06. Formal admissions rose to 27,700 in 2006–07 from 27,400 in 2005–06. The gap between formal admissions and the total detentions is as a result of informal patients being made subject to a detention order.*

- *92 per cent of all formal admissions in 2006–07 were to NHS hospitals*

- *87 per cent of all formal admissions were to NHS hospitals under Part 2 of the Act (the remainder were mostly through the courts). (www.ic.nhs.uk/webfiles/publications/inpatientsdetmha96to07/inpatients%20formally%20deta)*

Definition of mental disorder (Section 1(2))

For the first time a single broad definition of mental disorder applies throughout the Act and the previous categories of mental illness, mental impairment, severe mental impairment and psychopathic disorder have been abolished. This broad definition will mean that patient need rather than a diagnostic label should determine whether compulsion is required.

Learning disability

The new legislation preserves the effect of the Act as it applies to learning disability. The effect of abolishing the four categories of mental disorder will be that all the powers in the Act will in future apply to all types of mental disorder. There is a special provision which means that (as now) learning disability will only be treated as a mental disorder for those purposes if it is associated with abnormally aggressive or seriously irresponsible conduct on the part of the person concerned.

Powers to detain and treat people without their consent

As a social worker you are far more likely to come across people who have mental health problems and are receiving treatment (if any) in the community or who are in hospital on a voluntary or informal basis. However, the removal in certain circumstances of a patient's liberty is so serious that you need to understand both the process and the role of the various people who implement the appropriate sections of the legislation.

Article 5 of the European Convention on Human Rights protects patients against arbitrary detention and because of the seriousness of compulsory detention three safeguards exist.

- Except in an emergency the person must have a mental disorder that has been established on the basis of objective medical expertise.

- The mental disorder must warrant detention.

- Detention must continue only while the mental disorder persists. Therefore those carrying out the detention must review the situation at regular intervals to ensure that the criteria continue to be met.

With the above criteria in mind, it should be obvious that there needs to be a clear process to compulsorily admit someone to hospital. There are professionals who perform key tasks in the legislation, but first let us examine just who the major parties are.

Professionals and others concerned with the operation of the Act

The new legislation has broadened the group of professionals and others who can be involved in the operation of the Act. These are the approved mental health professional (AMHP), who replaces the former ASW and is the professional who applies for admission; the approved clinician (AC), who is a mental health practitioner – not restricted to just doctors – who for the purposes of the Act can make certain decisions about medical treatment that can be given without patient's consent. Significantly, only approved clinicians can go on to be Responsible Clinicians (RC), who replace the responsible medical officer (RMO) and who has the lead clinical responsibility for detained patients. The nearest relative is continued and can play an important part.

There are increased opportunities for social workers to become involved in a range of mental health work and even in the complex world of legislation social workers will be using their skills to communicate with people, help them to understand the challenges and problems they face and provide statutory bodies with reports and assessments.

What is an AMHP?

An AMHP or approved mental health professional is the replacement for the ASW or approved social worker. The key change with the new legislation is that this role is no longer confined to social workers. The government wanted AMHPs to be health professionals, which of course include social workers. AMHPs can be employed by local social services authorities (LSSAs) but could also be employed by NHS trusts or even be self-employed. Irrespective of their status the AMHP will be appointed to the role by an LSSA. He must exercise independent judgement and be personally accountable for his own practice and need not follow any directions that might be given to him by the LSSA.

Who can be an AMHP?

Existing approved social workers will become AMHPs overnight when the Act comes into force, probably in October 2008. LSSAs in conjunction with many universities are offering updating courses that will help prepare the newly converted AMHP for their role. These courses are endorsed by Skills for Care and approved by the GSCC. It is hoped that the new training will build on what was generally accepted as high-quality training for ASWs to ensure that the independence of the AMHP is maintained.

The role is now opened up to other professionals who have a range of experiences and skills in mental health including nurses, psychologists and occupational therapists and of course social workers but not doctors. It remains to be seen how effective this is and it does offer a different skill mix and a range of experiences. Arrangements for approvals are set out in the Mental Health (Approval of Persons to be Approved Mental Health Professionals) (England) Regulations 2008 ('the AMHP regulations').

Why have an AMHP?

The role of the AMHP is a direct replacement for the ASW and it is a requirement that the Local Social Services Authority (section 114 amended) appoint AMHPs who have an appropriate level of competence. AMHPs need not be employed by the LSSA and many will be working for NHS bodies.

AMHP functions including making applications for admission to hospital and guardianship applications, and agreeing that patients should become supervised community treatment patients (SCT).

The AMHP is pivotal to the admissions process and provides an important counterbalance to a more medicalised view of the individual's circumstances.

The AMHP is expected to:

- bring to any decision a separate perspective and model of mental health;
- provide a detailed and comprehensive understanding of social care and community resources;
- be able to assess social factors that provide the context in which the 'patient' is being seen;
- be able to carry out a comprehensive risk assessment;
- be trained to explore the least restrictive alternatives to any hospital admission;
- make the application to detain a patient founded on the recommendation of the doctor or doctors;
- organise and manage the practical aspects of assessments and if necessary admissions to hospital.

Nearest relative (NR)

This is an important role and safeguard under the MHA even though there has been considerable discussion as to whether this role should continue. The nearest relative has a range of functions in relation to patients who may be detained or liable to be detained under Part 2 of the MHA. These include the right to apply for compulsory admission or guardianship; be consulted before any application is made by an AMHP; within certain parameters object and stop any application for detention or guardianship; discharge the patient; apply to the Mental Health Review Tribunal for discharge; and receive information about the patient's and their own rights under the MHA.

Who is the nearest relative is determined according to a list which begins with husband, wife or civil partner, father then mother, etc. Amendments to the MHA 1983 made by MHA 2007 ensure that in the case of civil partners, one will be the nearest relative of the other, regardless of the length of their cohabitation (and even if they don't cohabit at all). Where there is more than one 'relative' it is the oldest who comes first. The nearest relative of a 'looked after child' is generally the local authority.

It is possible for a nearest relative to be displaced and this process involves application to the County Court (s.29). The AMHP may bring forward such an application and if successful it will be the local authority that is appointed as a NR. The amended Act makes it possible for a patient to make such an application and for a displacement order to be made on an additional ground; that the nearest relative is not a suitable person to act as a nearest relative.

Offences

Part 9 of the MHA identifies additional safeguards that were created to protect vulnerable individuals at the time when they are suffering with a mental disorder. This also means that failure to act appropriately could result in health and social care professionals facing civil or criminal proceedings if the quality of care and treatment falls short.

Independent mental health advocates

This was a last-minute concession by the government in order to secure enough votes to get the legislation through Parliament. However, the duty to arrange advocacy services (s.130A) is not expected to be in place until May 2009. Independent mental health advocates can help patients who are detained for treatment and those who are subject to guardianship or supervised community treatment.

Approved clinician (ACs)

This is an important new role that is not restricted to doctors and could include social workers. The role gives powers to detain inpatients for up to 72 hours (see s.5) in addition to the registered medical practitioner if the AC believes that an application for admission to hospital should be made. The AC may visit and assess patients at the request of the patient's nearest relative for a range of reasons including advice about powers of discharge or referral. The AC is expected to be competent to carry out assessments about the presence of and the nature of mental disorder, to be able to lead a multidisciplinary team and to be able to understand different treatment modalities and their applicability to a range of patients.

Responsible clinician (RCs)

This is the professional who has overall responsibility for decisions about the treatment of detained patients, a role that was formerly carried out by the responsible medical officer (RMO), who was of course a doctor. However, the new role of responsible clinician need not be filled by a doctor and could be a nurse, psychologist, an occupational therapist or a social worker, providing that they have undergone the appropriate specialist training. Before becoming a responsible clinician all professionals will need to have been an approved clinician. This is expected to be seen by these listed professionals as a career path position. This is an important change as for the first time in recent history the treatment and detention of patients lie in the hands of a range of professionals including but not limited to the medical profession.

The responsible clinician (RC) is defined in s.34 of the MHA 1983 as amended by MHA 2007.

Section 12 approved doctors

A section 12 doctor is a medical practitioner who has been approved under this section as a practitioner who has special interest and expertise in the diagnosis and treatment of mental disorder. Most family doctors do not have this level of understanding and experience and will be required to undertake specialist training before they can be appointed as a section 12 doctor.

Hospital managers

The hospital managers are by law the body responsible for detaining a patient under the MHA 1983. In a NHS hospital, the managers will be the NHS trust responsible for the hospital, and in an independent hospital it will be the person registered under the Care Standards Act 2000 in respect of that hospital. They must oversee the detaining documents to ensure that their treatment and care is in accord with the provisions of the specific section under which the patient is detained. They must also ensure that the patient has been informed of their rights and that as far as possible the patient understands such rights (with clear implications for people who cannot see, hear or for whom English is not a comprehensible language).

Admission to hospital (compulsory detention)

As a social worker you need to understand what happens to patients when they are detained in hospital, what to advise their carers and what they should expect from the hospital and community services. Having described the key people concerned with the compulsory detention of patients, it is now necessary to see what part they play in such a decision. Basically in every compulsory 'civil' admission process the AMHP or the nearest relative makes the application on the prescribed form (which is a statutory form) which is founded upon at least one medical recommendation. Neither party on their own can admit a patient to hospital. To help to make this clearer, let us identify some key decision-making points.

- Does the patient have the capacity to make a judgement about their condition?

- If the answer to the above is no, are they resisting going into hospital?

- If the answer is that they do have capacity to make their own decisions, are they willing to go into hospital on their own volition?

- If they are not willing to go into hospital, are the circumstances such that they will meet legal criteria that will permit compulsory admission?

- If the answer is no, then no admission will occur but community services and support should be mobilised.

- If the answer is that the patient does meet the criteria for compulsory admission, is this a situation which would be classed as an emergency?

- If the patient meets the criteria for admission, do we know what the nature and extent of the mental disorder are or do we need an assessment to be carried out?

- If the patient meets the criteria for admission and we know the nature and extent of the mental disorder, is there treatment available at the hospital?

This is complex, as the deprivation of anyone's human rights as a compulsory detention should be a last resort and in line with the principles that underpin the legislation. The following case study should help to understand how such questions are addressed.

CASE STUDY

This is a long case study that if you work through will help you to understand the process that lies behind Part 2 admissions or civil admissions.

There is a summary table shortly after this case study (Table 3.1) that shows the differences between the main sections of the Act under Part 2.

Susan is a 17-year-old about whom her parents have become increasingly concerned. She has been acting strangely by staying up all night and sleeping throughout the day. This has gone on for a couple of weeks and there has been a marked deterioration in her behaviour since she last saw her family GP, who had prescribed her some antidepressants. The family were struggling to cope with this behaviour but now had found some notes that they took as intent to seriously harm herself. She flew into a rage when she discovered that they had been in her room reading her notes and opening up her emails on her computer.

The doctor has now arrived and Susan has shut herself in her room and is screaming and throwing stuff around the room. She is shouting abuse and threatening to kill herself if anyone comes near her. The doctor is confused as to what to do next but thinks admission to the local psychiatric unit would be appropriate.

What is the next step?

This is a tricky situation but let us work through the key decision points mentioned earlier.

First, does she have capacity? By all accounts, when she is calmer she is perfectly capable of understanding information that is related to the decision about her situation and would be able to retain this information and to weigh up the alternatives. In other words, she would almost certainly be deemed to be able to make a decision about whether she should go into hospital, and therefore is not an incapable person within the meaning of the MCA. The result of this is that the initial decision to use either the MHA or the MCA is now firmly on the side of using the MHA.

Is Susan resisting going to hospital? This is difficult to say as she is in such a state that communication is difficult, but as far as the doctor can determine she will not go anywhere, let alone a hospital.

Next, does she have a mental disorder of a nature or degree that warrants detention in hospital for a least a limited period? Her family GP has of course been treating her for depression and has prescribed a course of antidepressants. Does this mean that she has a mental disorder that is so serious as to warrant detention in hospital? It does not if this was the only evidence but the latest outburst and the worsening of her behaviour may indicate that she might meet the criteria. Let's suppose that on balance the GP thinks she does meet the criteria for a mental disorder. This alone is not enough. Susan must now meet the grounds that she ought to be detained in the interests of her own health or safety or with a view to the protection of others. This too is a judgement call and if this ground or condition is not met, no admission can proceed against her wishes.

Is the situation a genuine emergency? This is important because in an emergency a patient may be admitted to hospital on the basis of a single medical recommendation providing that the applicant (either the AMHP or the NR) agrees. If it would cause 'undesirable delay' to wait for a second recommendation, section 4 allows the patient to be detained for up to 72 hours while that recommendation is sought. Remember that most family GPs are not mental health specialists. If, within the 72-hour period, a second medical recommendation is obtained, the patient will be deemed to be detained under section 2 (and to have been so from the point at which they was first admitted under section 4). If this situation can wait (there are time limits) the doctor needs to decide to use either a section 2 or a section 3 admission.

Let us assume that the doctor decides that although in his view an admission is necessary, he thinks it better and more appropriate for this to be a section 2, which is for assessment followed by treatment if necessary. His justification would be that as no one knows what the nature of the mental disorder is, an assessment is needed and at this stage the exact nature of any treatment is unknown. The existing antidepressant medication appears ineffective. If Susan is to be admitted under section 2, the two doctors need to make their recommendation and either the AMHP or the nearest relative needs to make the actual application.

It is likely that the applicant will be the AMHP rather than the nearest relative and many professionals think that this would be more appropriate given that at some point Susan will return back to the family. The AMHP plays a key role as they will be the applicant and without them no admission will occur. The AMHP has an independent decision to make and they are required to consider the relative merits of admission taking into account the principle of the 'least restrictive alternative'. The AMHP must also take into account the views of the nearest relative about admission and if the AMHP decides not to go ahead they must explain to the NR in writing why they have made this decision and what the alternatives proposed are.

If the application goes ahead the AMHP must arrange and co-ordinate the assessment and this will include the arrangements to take Susan to the hospital. The draft revised Code of Practice is clear that although AMHPs act as independent professionals they must exercise their judgement based on the evidence that is available and to take into account the availability of community alternatives (DoH, Mental Health Act 1983, draft Revised Code of Practice (2007) Para 4.4).

How does the AMHP make this assessment? It is the duty of the AMHP to interview the patient in a *suitable manner* and to satisfy him or herself that *in all the circumstances of the case it is the most appropriate way of providing the care and treatment* which Susan needs. But how does he achieve this when Susan has shut herself in her room and is screaming and shouting? This is where the experience and the skill of the AMHP will come into play to try to get to interview Susan. Carrying out an interview through a closed door would not be considered as a suitable manner. Let us assume that through a combination of persistence and skill the AMHP has interviewed Susan and she remains agitated and still threatening to self-harm. Two doctors have seen her, including a section 12 approved one, and they are recommending admission to hospital.

CASE STUDY *continued*

The AMHP has now completed the application process founded on the two doctors' recommendations and now the ambulance has arrived to convey Susan to hospital.

What happens next?

Applicants for compulsory admission under Part 2, irrespective of who is the applicant, are authorised by s.6(1) to take and convey or to authorise others to so do. In this case the AMHP has authorised the ambulance staff to carry out this responsibility. While they are doing this they have the power of a constable including arresting any person who is wilfully obstructing them. The conveyance to hospital has to be lawful and humane and if the patient is likely to be troublesome the AMHP should give advice and assistance.

In the unlikely event of Susan escaping, the person who had the patient in legal custody has the power under s.18 to retake them into custody with a view to satisfactorily reconveying them to hospital.

CASE STUDY *continued*

Susan has now arrived at the hospital. What should happen next?

It is important to note that a child is defined as anyone who is under 18 years old. There is no age limit for the application of the MHA although guardianship cannot be used where the patient is under 16. There is a new duty to provide suitable age-related accommodation under s.31 of the MHA; therefore Susan should not be admitted to an adult ward. In cases where a child or adolescent is concerned, at least one of the applicants or doctors should have specialist child or adolescent knowledge.

Applications for compulsory admission are addressed to the hospital manager and it therefore falls to them to ensure that the grounds for admission are valid and that all the paperwork is complete. In addition there is a quality-assurance role in that periodically all documents must be audited and those responsible must be aware of the sorts of errors that are able to be rectified and those that cannot be changed. The hospital manager also has the legal responsibility to inform patients of their right to advocacy and their rights to appeal to the mental health review tribunal where this is relevant. In some cases, information must also be provided to the patient's nearest relative. These steps must be taken as soon as practicable after admission and should be repeated if there is any doubt that the patient has fully comprehended the information.

If Susan's nearest relative had made the application (her father?) then the hospital manager is required to let the LSSA know as soon as practicable. Once this information is received the LSSA will direct an AMHP to visit and prepare a social circumstances report which is forwarded to the managers.

Having worked through a section 2 admission you should by now have got the general idea about the legal process of admission and some of the issues that may arise during such processes. The next step is to look at some of the other more commonly used parts of the legislation which are all variants of the section 2 admission process. These are summarised in Table 3.1.

Table 3.1: *The compulsory admission process to hospital: Summary of main provisions*

	Section 2 (assessment)	Section 3 (treatment)	Section 4 (emergency)
What is it?	Provides for admission for those who have a mental disorder that warrants detention. Interests of their health or safety or protection of others	For those who are suffering from a mental disorder and it is necessary for their health or safety or for the protection of others and that this cannot be provided without detention and that the appropriate treatment is available.	To be used only in an emergency and where unnecessary delay would be caused by waiting for a second medical recommendation
What is the effect?	Length of detention is up to 28 days and cannot be extended	Up to six months initially and can be renewed for a further six, then in periods of one year	Up to 72 hours. Can be converted to s.2 providing second doctor recommends and applicant agrees
Process	Nearest relative or AMHP is the applicant. Plus two doctors, one of whom must be s.12 approved	NR or AMHP is the applicant. Plus two doctors, one of whom must be s.12 approved	NR or AMHP plus one doctor who ideally should know the patient and should only be used where it is an emergency
Notes	This is the section by which those whose mental disorder is uncertain would be admitted under	This is the 'main' section by which patients are admitted to hospital to have treatment	With this section the patient is deprived of a fundamental safeguard in that the doctor who recommends need not have specialist mental health knowledge

Applications for admission for assessment or treatment may be made for patients who are already in hospital.

Holding powers pending applications in respect of patients already in hospital (sections 5(2) and 5(4))

In certain circumstances, informal inpatients may be detained temporarily in the hospital pending the making of an application, as described below. This does not apply to patients who are already detained on the basis of an application under the Act, or to SCT patients. There are two main powers, one for doctors and the other for certain prescribed nurses.

Holding power of doctor or approved clinician in charge of patient's treatment (s.5(2))

Inpatients can be detained in a hospital for up to 72 hours if the doctor or approved clinician in charge of their treatment reports that an application for admission under section 2 or 3 ought to be made.

Nurses' six-hour holding power (s.5(4))

Nurses 'of the prescribed class' may authorise the detention for up to six hours of a patient who is already being treated for mental disorder in the hospital as an inpatient if they think that:

- The patient is suffering from mental disorder to such a degree that it is necessary for the patient's health or safety or for the protection of others, for the patient to be immediately restrained from leaving the hospital; and it is not practicable to secure the immediate attendance of a doctor or an approved clinician.

Compulsory powers in the community

Community patients and supervised community treatment (SCT)

One of the more controversial elements of the new law is the new community measure called supervised community treatment (SCT) under which a community treatment order (CTO) may be imposed upon a patient who is already liable to be detained. SCT is a new measure for those who are eligible for community treatment and who need supervision. This is described in detail in the draft MHA reference guide to the Act. There is the possibility of considerable confusion here as most patients in the community are not subject to any legislative device and could legitimately be described as 'community patients'. For those, and it is thought that this will be a relatively small number, on a CTO under supervision they will be able to live in the community under the powers of the Mental Health Act, to ensure they continue with the medical treatment that they need.

To be eligible for SCT a patient must be liable to be detained under s.3 of Part 2 or a hospital order or a transfer direction under Part 3 of the Act and who, without continued treatment, would be a risk to their own health or safety or that of others. A CTO will be made by the RC with the written agreement of an AMHP. The initial period will be for six months with renewal at six months and thereafter annually.

Fennell suggests that there are disturbing features of this new power from a human rights perspective as the conditions and restrictions on personal freedom is left to the professional discretion of health professionals (Fennel, 2007, p212). But concerns over this measure might be due to the fact that the orders are a leap into the unknown. Despite being used in other parts of the world, in some cases for decades, there is little evidence that they work. This is the worrying conclusion arrived at by a Department of Health-funded analysis published in March 2007. Rachel Churchill and colleagues from the Institute of Psychiatry in London analysed all available research on such orders in North America and Australasia (28 reports of outcome studies on such orders). Their conclusion was: *There is very little evidence to suggest that CTOs are associated with any positive outcomes and there is justification for further research in this area.* Faced with this report, the government has commissioned a major research study (circa £500,000) led by the University of Oxford to determine the effectiveness of CTOs in the early stages of implementation.

Leave of absence (s.17)

Section 17 leave was originally intended as a measure that would allow detained patients to go home for short periods or to go out to shops nearby to the hospital to help determine if they were ready to be discharged from hospital. However, no restrictions were made on the length of this leave. With the arrival of the CTO this should replace the longer-term uses of s.17 leave. Indeed, where an RC is proposing to give a detained patient leave of seven days duration or more, he may do so only if he has first considered imposing a CTO on the patient.

Responsible after-care bodies (s.117(3))

The duty to provide after-care services under section 117 stands by itself. It is not a duty to provide services under other legislation (e.g. the National Assistance Act 1948 or the NHS Act 2006). As a result, normal rules about commissioning responsibility (in the NHS) or ordinary residence (for social services) do not apply. The consequence of this is that the responsible after-care bodies are the LSSA and the PCT for the area in which the person concerned is resident or is sent on discharge by the hospital in which the patient was detained.

Guardianship

Guardianship orders can be either a civil process (Part 2) or can be made through the courts (Part 3). The consequences of a guardianship order are set out in Table 3.2. The main provision is that guardianship may be used to restrict patients' liberty (e.g. by determining where they are to live) but it may not be used to deprive them of their liberty (i.e. to detain them).

If the patient lacks the capacity to make a decision for themself and their best interests would be to reside in a hospital or care home, and to be deprived of liberty there, it may be necessary to use the DoLS procedure in order to obtain an appropriate authorisation under the MCA. If such patients require treatment for mental disorder in hospital and they object to being admitted, it might be necessary to admit (or transfer) them to hospital under the MHA.

Part 2 Civil orders

Although this has not been used anything like the extent to which it was envisaged, it remains a less restrictive alternative to hospital detention. The range of patients eligible has been extended and with powers generally contained in Part 2 of the Act it is expected that more orders will be made. Either the AMHP or the nearest relative can apply to have a person made subject to a guardianship order. The patient must have a mental disorder of a nature or degree that warrants guardianship and it must be in the interests of the patient's welfare or for the protection of others.

Part 3 Court-made orders

The offender being considered for guardianship must be over 16 years of age and have a mental disorder of a nature or degree that warrants guardianship. The court decides if guardianship is suitable and will take into account all the circumstances of the case. Importance will be placed on reports made to the courts and the LSSA will be able to let the court know if it is prepared to receive the order and how it can exercise its responsibilities to the offender. The medical evidence is the same as for a civil order.

Care Programme Approach (CPA)

At present all mental health service users are entitled to the Care Programme Approach, which has two levels. However, in practice this has meant that mostly only those entitled to an enhanced level of CPA actually received a service. From 1 October 2008 the CPA will only apply to those at this level but will include all patients who are currently or have been recently detained under the MHA. This is called a 'refocused' CPA and the National Director for Mental Health in the forward of *Refocusing the CPA* stated the rationale as:

> the Care Programme Approach (CPA) is at the centre of a personalisation process, supporting individuals with severe mental illness to ensure their needs and choices remain central in what are often complex systems of care.
> (DoH, 2008).

Service users eligible for CPA can expect:

- support from a trained CPA co-ordinator;
- a comprehensive multi-agency and multi-disciplinary assessment covering the full range of needs and risks;
- an assessment of their financial needs including direct payments;
- a comprehensive written care plan including risk assessments and contingency measures;
- the need for advocacy services assessed;
- at review consideration for ongoing CPA support;
- carers informed of their rights to their own assessment.

One of the consequences of the increasing complexity of systems of care and treatment is that they can become disjointed. Consequently a new shared computerised record system between primary and secondary care is scheduled to come into practice by 2010.

Table 3.2: *Summary of main compulsory powers in the community*

	Section 117	Section 17	SCT or CTO (comes into force October 2008)	Section 7 Guardianship
What is it?	Places a duty on the PCT and LSSA to provide after-care for patients who have been detained on any order specifying treatment, e.g. s. 3 or s. 37	Enables the RC to grant leave for a detained patient to reside in the community, during which time the patient agrees to treatment that can include taking medication as a condition for discharge. Failure to comply can result in readmission to hospital	Eligible patients are those who are liable to be detained in a hospital or if a Part 3 patient be subject to a hospital order. A patient on this order will be known as a community patient. The treatment must be available in the community and it must be necessary for the patient's health or safety or for the protection of others that he receives this treatment.	An order that is less restrictive than being detained in hospital while retaining the same powers under Part 2. Patients must be over 16 years of age. It was thought that this section would herald a move towards more care in the community but the small number of orders actually made suggest otherwise
What is the effect?	Imposes a duty on the local authority to assess a patient for eligibility for community services	Although the patient must agree to treatment in the community there is no provision whereby the patient can be made to accept treatment including medication	Patient must reside at an agreed address, be available for treatment and receive it. Patient must abstain from particular behaviours. Note the obligation to receive medical treatment, which is stronger than in s.17	Three powers are conferred on the guardian (s.8). The patient must reside at an agreed address; attend for treatment; and allow access to address of certain specified persons. Where the court makes the order it in effect assumes the role of the applicant
The process	The duty applies when the patient who is liable to be detained is discharged from hospital. Patients who are on SCT are also entitled to be assessed for community services under this section	The RC can grant indefinite leave or more frequently leave for a specified length of time, which must be more than seven days. The RC must have considered the merits of a Community Treatment Order before using this section	The RC can order the willing discharge of an eligible patient who will be subject to recall if the patient does not comply with their treatment (ss17 and 17E). Before an order can be made the AMHP must agree and do so in writing. The order can be renewed (s.20A). The initial period will be for six months with renewal at six months and thereafter annually	Either the nearest relative or the AMHP can apply plus two medical recommendations. If an AMHP makes the application the NR can object although if thought unreasonable this objection can be overruled by a County Court.
notes	Section 117 services are provide under the remit of s.46 of the NHS and CCA 1990 and requires that the LSSA carries out a two-stage assessment of needs for services. Once assessed as needing services the LSSA cannot charge for these services	This was designed to reduce the numbers of patients who were considered to be revolving-door patients. It allows the patient to leave hospital while still being subject to the powers of the Act. Non-compliant patients can be recalled and once back at hospital can be made subject to a CTO. Recalling automatically revokes the leave	This replaces supervised discharge under s.25A-25J which was seldom used. These came into force after a series of cases that were high profile and showed that community care was not working. The new community treatment orders are referred to in the MHA 2007 as supervised community treatment. The patient can be recalled for up to 72 hours without affecting the order. Longer than this and the patient reverts to a detained patient status	Although this order can be used for Part 2 and Part 3 patients, mostly it is used in civil circumstances. The numbers of guardianship orders may increase as the new law broadens the power and extends the range of people to whom it might apply

Patients concerned in criminal proceedings or under sentence

The provisions in Part 3 of the Act enable the courts to order that offenders be detained in hospital for treatment, rather than prison.

Hospital orders (s. 37 and s. 41)

A small number of people may be admitted to hospital from the Crown Court. This may be pursuant to a Hospital Order made under section 37 of the MHA (for example), following their conviction for a criminal offence, or it may be as a result of their pleading that their mental state makes it impossible for them to have a fair trial. In the latter case, the patient will be subject to a Hospital Order by virtue of the Criminal Procedure (Insanity and Unfitness to Plead) Act 1991.

Where the court has convicted a person they can be remanded for psychiatric reports for up to 12 weeks before sentencing. Where mental disorder is apparent at the time of sentencing they may be admitted to a hospital under section 37 which is similar in extent to section 3 except that the applicant is in effect the Courts. If when making a Hospital Order, the Court decides that the public need protection from serious harm it may also make a Restriction Order under section 41. The effect of a Restriction Order is that in most cases, the patient may not be discharged from hospital, transferred to another hospital or granted leave without the permission of the Secretary of State.

The concept of social vulnerability comes into play when a crime involves an older person who has limited capacity perhaps caused by mental illness or dementia. There are now a range of new offences under s.44 Mental Capacity Act 2005 (ill treatment or wilful neglect of a person who lacks capacity) and s.4 Fraud Act 2006 (this is called fraud by abuse of position).

> **KEY FACTS**
>
> *Court and prison disposals were 1,900 in 2006–07, the same as in 1996–97, and have risen 11 per cent compared to 2005–06 (1,700).*
>
> (Source: The Information Centre for Social Care)

Treatment in hospital or the community

Medical treatment means a range of interventions including drug treatments, nursing care and therapeutic interventions, and could include behaviour modification and task-centred work. Where medical treatment is given, it should only be for the mental disorder that the patient is suffering. This provides a degree of safeguard for the patient but is open to interpretation and professional discretion. When a patient's life is under threat, the situation is far more complex. For example, the treatment of patients who have chronic eating disorders may necessitate 'forced' feeding, which is a physical treatment for a condition widely considered to have a psychological component. Where to draw the line between physical and mental disorder is usually a matter for professional decision-making and rulings through the courts. It is assumed that every adult patient has capacity to consent unless they lack capacity to make the decision, as defined in the MCA 2005.

Drug treatment

Patients who are detained under the MHA 1983 are subject to the provisions of Part 4 of the Act, which covers treatments that require consent and a second opinion (s.57), which is usually psycho-surgery; treatment that requires consent or a second opinion (s.58), usually medicine for a patient's mental disorder; and urgent treatment (s.62), which justifies departure from the requirements of s.58. The implications for practice are to be found in the Code of Practice. Medicine can be given to patients who are detained for treatment under s.3 or a hospital order (s.37) without their consent or a second opinion, for up to three months. This is known as the 'three month rule'. After three months, such treatment can only be given if its use has been approved by a second opinion appointed doctor (SOAD).

The medical treatment of informal patients in psychiatric hospitals in many ways mirrors that of patients in general hospitals and if they have the requisite capacity, such patients have the right to refuse treatment as well as discharge themselves without conditions (subject to s.5 holding powers). As the vast majority of capable patients are informal, the common law applies to their treatment for mental disorder in the same way as any other health problem. This means that every patient has the individual right to refuse treatment even if that refusal may be injurious to his or her health. Under the MCA, an incapable patient who is not detained under the MHA may be given medical treatment that includes treatment for a mental disorder that is considered to be in their best interests.

However, the situation for patients who are subject to the detention powers in the MHA 1983 is different as they may in certain conditions be made to have treatment even though they object strongly to this form of intervention. The authority for this can be found in Part 4 of the MHA 1983, which applies only to detained patients. The policy of overriding the patient's wishes is justified when it is in either or both the patient's best interest or for the good of others. Although the use of such measures is provided with safeguards such as a second opinion, it is nevertheless seen by some as an example of the social-control function of psychiatry.

Elsewhere the range of medical interventions is discussed (Chapter 2). It is worth reflecting that prescribed drugs for the treatment of mental disorder account for around 25 per cent of all prescriptions issued through the NHS (Bartlett and Sandland, 2003, 326). The treatment of a chronic disorder like schizophrenia is estimated to be over £1 billion pounds alone. Even with this huge spend, patients report varying degrees of satisfaction with these medications and relapse rate continues to be at a level that stretches service-level provision and the side-effects cause some distress to many users.

For patients who are on SCT it is likely that their order will specify that they must continue to have treatment as directed by the RC and in particular to take prescribed medication.

Electro-convulsive treatment (ECT)

This treatment involves giving the patient electric shock treatment and is still in widespread use and usually considered when drug regimes appear not to work. It is an established method of treating people who have depression affective psychoses. ECT is always administered under anaesthetic and a muscle relaxant. Electrodes are placed on the temple and then a short electric shock is administered which produces a convulsion similar to an epileptic fit. Why this works for some patients and not for others remains a matter for speculation.

Many patients consent to this treatment but where patients do not and are detained they can, with certain safeguards, be given ECT against their wishes. Except in an emergency, a patient who is detained under the MHA but capable of consenting to ECT may only be given it with his consent. In the case of an incapable detained patient, ECT may only be given if it has been approved by a SOAD. If the patient is under 16 years of age and the situation is not considered urgent, SOAD approval will be required whether the patient is capable or incapable, and even if he isn't detained under the MHA. The length of treatment is usually 6 or 12 courses of treatment and approximately 20,000 patients have this treatment every year in the UK. Side-effects can include memory impairment, often temporary, and confusion. Among older patients there are risks of strokes and heart attacks (Openmind, 1985). There is a possibility that the use of ECT against the wishes of detained patients contravenes the Human Rights Act but to date no legal action has been brought.

Psychosurgery

Although quite common at one time, with over 10,000 operations performed, this is now seldom carried out and when it is, it is subject to the investigation of a panel appointed by the Mental Health Act Commission and requires the patient's consent. Psychosurgery is irreversible.

Emergency treatment

This can mean the administration of medications and/or the restraint or seclusion of patients who are liable to be detained while in hospital. This is provided under s. 62 and is limited to the minimum treatment necessary to respond to the emergency. This may not always be dramatic life-saving situations but could be for 'lesser emergencies'. Evidence suggests that from time to time this section has been used to include patients who are in hospital informally and presenting difficult behaviour on the hospital wards (Bartlett and Sandham, 2003).

Restraint may be necessary from time to time and should only be carried out by trained staff who are able to exercise minimal force that is consistent with resolution of the behaviour. The use of restraint is controversial and dates back to the use of straightjackets and other mechanical restraints. In the present time investigations and inquiries have thrown doubt upon the capabilities of some staff (MHAC, 2001).

When a patient's behaviour warrants it, he/she can be placed in seclusion, which involves the patient remaining in a room that is specially designated for the purpose that meets certain minimum requirements. While in this room the ward staff are required to not only observe the patient but also to record these observations and to arrange for medical review at periodic intervals. The MHAC reviews the use of seclusion and reports on this from time to time.

Part 9 offences

It is an offence for any person employed in a hospital or care home to ill-treat or wilfully neglect a patient who is receiving treatment as an inpatient or community patient (this includes guardianship). The penalty has recently been increased to a term not exceeding five years imprisonment, which reflects the seriousness of this sort of offence and how it is viewed.

Part 10 Miscellaneous and supplementary

Under sections 135 and 136 of the Mental Health Act 1983 a police officer may remove a person who is believed or appears to be suffering from a mental disorder to a place of safety. Section 44 of the 2007 Act amends these sections of the 1983 Act to allow a person to be taken from one place of safety to one or more other places of safety during the 72-hour maximum overall period during which they may be detained under either of these two sections. This can be carried out by a police officer, an approved social worker (until approved social workers are replaced by AMHPs) or someone authorised by either of them (Mental Health Act 2007 (Commencement No.5 and Transitional Provisions) Order 2008).

Getting out of hospital
Discharge

Informal patients cannot be subjected to compulsions of any kind and they may leave hospital when they wish (subject to the holding powers of s.5 of the MHA). In practice, patients should be advised to discuss discharge with their RC and others once they begin to feel better; this may be when medication has begun to work or when circumstances at home or in the community would allow them to leave hospital. This may necessitate social workers becoming involved in order to identify support services and systems that could be available for the patient and their families.

In some circumstances, a patient may be discharged from detention by his nearest relative (see s.23 of the MHA). It might, however be possible for the responsible clinician (RC) to bar the patient's discharge, provided he does so in writing and within 72 hours of receipt of the nearest relatives order (s.25(1) MHA).

A detained patient may apply for his discharge to the hospital managers and/or to the Mental Health Review Tribunal. A patient can seek discharge from both and being unsuccessful in one should not preclude success in the other.

Hospital managers review

When a patient is detained under the MHA 1983 they can request that the hospital managers review the reasons for their continuing detention. Hospitals appoint a range of people who have had training and who have experience to act in this capacity. If the managers decide that the applicant is not suffering from a mental disorder or that he/she could live back in the community, they can order the discharge of the patient.

Mental health review tribunal (s.65)

Mental health review tribunals (MHRT) are independent judicial bodies with the power to decide if a patient should continue to be formally detained or continue to be subject to supervised community treatment. Despite its name, this tribunal does not review the original decision to detain patients. In coming to a decision the tribunal has to make a balanced judgement, often weighing up the rights of the individual against the best interests of the individual and public protection. The hospital managers (NHS trust or independent hospital registered to take detained patients) or if subject to guardianship, the local social services authority (LSSA), must justify the need for the continued use of the Act. The Act sets out the circumstances in which an MHRT can discharge a detained patient. When granting a patient his discharge, the MHRT has the power to defer the date on which it will take effect. Alternatively, and with a view to facilitating a patient's discharge in the future, the MHRT may recommend that he be given leave of absence, transferred to another hospital or into guardianship, or be made subject to SCT. Each MHRT has three members: a legal member who is its president, a medical member who is usually a consultant psychiatrist, and a lay member. All members are appointed by the Ministry of Justice. Each member must consider the case on its individual merits.

Social workers should always remind the patient that they are entitled to be represented by a solicitor with specialist mental health experience, absolutely free of charge under the legal aid scheme. This is especially important as the patient/NR may be worried about paying the fee. The solicitor may decide to involve an expert witness, e.g. independent psychiatrist, social worker or psychologist. In the case of long-term patients detained under s.3 who do not apply to the tribunal within the first six months, the hospital manager must refer the case to the tribunal.

In most cases a social circumstances report will be required and these can be compiled by a social worker who need not be an AMHP. Over recent years there has been some concern about the quality and information contained in some social circumstances reports. The information required by the tribunal in respect of these reports are to be found in the 1983 MHRT Rules 32(1) Schedule 1, Pt. B, Para 2, which include providing an up-to-date report with information on:

- the patient's home and family circumstances including the attitude of the nearest relative or the person so acting;

- any opportunities for employment and the housing and other facilities that the patient would be able to use if discharged;

- what community support and medical facilities are available;
- the financial circumstances of the patient.

The future of regulation

The Health and Social Care Bill 2007 is before Parliament and includes measures to abolish the present regulatory and inspection body known as the Mental Health Act Commission (MHAC) and transfer its functions (in relation to England) to the new Care Quality Commission which will provide an integrated approach to regulation of the sector. The plan is that the Commission will be up and running in 2009 and fully operational by 2010. This will establish a 'super regulator' by combining the functions of the Healthcare Commission, Commission for Social Care Inspection and the Mental Health Act Commission. This regulator will operate a 'light touch' for most providers but where significant failings are discovered will have the power to close wards or services. The important role of the Mental Health Act Commission in visiting patients detained under the Mental Health Act 1983 will be retained but it remains unclear whether it will continue to have the wider role it has forged in the protection of patients deprived of their liberty. The effectiveness of this 'super regulator' remains to be seen.

C H A P T E R   S U M M A R Y

This chapter has introduced you to the complex area of law and the inevitable responsibilities that are placed upon professionals. To deprive someone of their liberty is so serious that legal safeguards are essential. The new provision of the AMHP has been looked at in depth and through the case study you have covered one of the main processes through which people can be admitted to hospital even if they object. Although some of the roles are specialised, it is essential that all social workers understand the basic provisions of the Mental Health Act and the Mental Capacity Act and their corresponding Codes of Practice. Remember that all law is experimental and subject to interpretation and change –it is your responsibility as a professional to keep up-to-date.

FURTHER READING

Fennell, P. (2007) Mental health: The new law. Bristol: Jordan Publishing.

This is an excellent reference book. If you are interested in becoming an AMHP this is a key text for you study.

For the Mental Health Act 2007 itself, see:

Department of Health (2008) *Mental Health Act 1983 Draft Reference Guide to the Mental Health Act 1983 as amended by the Mental Health Act 2007*. Can be downloaded (beware: over 300 pages) *from* www.dh.gov.uk/publications

For a scholarly discussion of Community Treatment Orders set alongside the findings from a systematic review of existing studies on Community Treatment Orders, a report well worth reading is the report by King's College London, Institute of Psychiatry (2007), *International Experiences of using Community Treatment Orders*, which can be obtained either on the web or from the Section of Evidence-based Mental Health, Health Services Research Department, PO Box 32, Institute of Psychiatry, King's College London, De Crespigny Park, London SE5 8AF. Their web address is: www.iop.kcl.ac.uk/news/downloads/Final2CTOReport8March07.pdf

For the hungry statistician, your first port of call should be the Information Centre for Social Care. They provide an annual publication which summarises information about people detained under the 1983 Mental Health Act in NHS facilities, including high-security psychiatric hospitals, and independent hospitals. It includes figures for the period 1996–97 to 2006–07. Their web address is www.ic.nhs.uk/ statistics-and-data-collections/mental-health/mental-health-act/in-patients

Chapter 4

Working with vulnerable people: mental health in children and adolescents

There is always one moment in childhood when the door opens and lets the future in.
Graham Greene (1940)

A C H I E V I N G   A   S O C I A L   W O R K   D E G R E E

This chapter will help you to meet the following National Occupational Standards.
Key Role 1: Prepare for and work with individuals, families, carers, groups and communities to assess their needs and circumstances
- Assess needs and options to recommend a course of action.

Key Role 2: Plan, carry out, review and evaluate social work practice, with individuals, families, carers, groups and communities and other professionals
- Interact with individuals, families, carers, groups and communities to achieve change and development and to improve life opportunities.
- Address behaviour which presents a risk to individuals, families, carers, groups and communities.

Key Role 6: Demonstrate professional competence in social work practice
- Research, analyse, evaluate and use current knowledge of best social work practice.
- Work within agreed standards of social work practice and ensure own professional development.

It will also introduce you to the following academic standards as set out in the subject benchmark statement which includes:

4.3 Defining Principles
There are competing views in society at large on the nature of social work and on its place and purpose. Social work practice and education inevitably reflect these differing perspectives on the role of social work in relation to social justice, social care and social order.

5.1.1 Social work services, service users and carers, which include:
- The nature of social work services in a diverse society (with particular reference to concepts such as prejudice, interpersonal, institutional and structural discrimination, empowerment and anti-discriminatory practices).
- The nature and validity of different definitions of, and explanations for, the characteristics and circumstances of service users and the services required by them, drawing on knowledge from research, practice experience, and from service users and carers.
- The focus on outcomes, such as promoting the well-being of young people and their families, and promoting dignity, choice and independence for adults receiving services.

5.1.2 The service delivery context
The issues and trends in modern public and social policy and their relationship to contemporary practice and service delivery in social work.
The significance of interrelationships with other social services, especially education, housing, health, income maintenance and criminal justice.
The current range and appropriateness of statutory, voluntary and private agencies providing community-based, day-care, residential and other services and the organisational systems inherent within these.

Introduction

In this chapter you will consider the kind of issues and knowledge that social workers need in order to carry out effective work with children and adolescents who have poor mental health. This will help you to understand the nature of these mental health problems and disorders and how to respond to them. Later on the focus is on working with adolescents who are dealing with the problems of eating disorders, self-harm, dissociative disorder and depression.

The government undertook a crucial policy initative under the general heading of Every Child Matters, which will transform children's services, The Children Act 2004 provides the legal framework for improving children's lives. The government state that it 'is to encourage integrated planning, commissioning and delivery of services as well as improve the coordination of individual and joint inspections in local authorites. The legislation is enabling rather than prescriptive and provides local authoriteis with a considerable amount of flexibility in the way they implement its provisions'. (www.dfes.gov.uk)

What social workers need to know to work effectively with children and adolescents

Social work with children and adolescents has until recently received little attention. However the government has endorsed the need for community and specialist services for this important group. Social workers have the skills necessary to work effectively with adolescents and to be key workers in multi-disciplinary settings.

There are many approaches that social workers and others use, some more effective than others. All have behind them a set of assumptions that raise issues for you, the service user and their carers. For example when working with an adolescent who displays behaviour associated with depression is the adolescent the primary client or is it the worried parent? Working with the adolescent to help them to articulate their needs may be at odds with what their family want and believe should happen. A child may be bottling up feelings because they inwardly feel that to open up is to risk alienation of the family, yet it may be in their interests to express these feelings.

As a social worker you need to understand what the various mental disorders are in order that you can work alongside other professionals as well as undertaking direct work yourself. This is a complex area and you need to resist making simplistic assessments of complex situations and playing the role of amateur psychiatrist. Where your strengths lie is in using an empowering approach when you can work with people to help them discover explanations that they understand and ways of intervening that actually work for them. The real experts are the service users who have experienced for themselves the impact of mental disorder.

You could be working with children, adolescents and families as part of a team or approach or in your own right. The kind of problems that you could be working with can be categorised as follows:

Under -5s

- communication problems;
- sleeping difficulties;
- unusually strong or long-lasting tantrums;
- children who are suffering anxieties after major trauma or major life events such as divorce or separation of parents.

School-age but pre-adolescent children

- hyperactive problems;
- bed-wetting or soiling;
- relationship problems;
- behavioural problems at home or school;
- school refusal problems.

Adolescents

- eating disorders;
- behavioural problems;
- anxiety states;
- self-harm;
- depression;
- substance abuse.

Of course before social workers get involved these problems and disorders must be perceived as either dysfunctional or disruptive and therefore it is essential to determine if this behaviour is within 'normal' or acceptable limits. Being in a position to do this requires that you have an understanding of the usual progression of children and adolescents and some knowledge of the kind of mental health problems and mental disorder that young people face. There are some disorders that are more closely associated with children and adolescents, even though they may also occur in adults.

Definitions of mental health in the context of adolescent development

Chapter 2 covered the main elements that make up a diagnosis of mental disorder and help us to appreciate mental health problems. It is worth revisiting this in the context of children and adolescents as there is a view held by many people that what we see as mental health problems are, in effect, simply signs of growing up that all of us have experience of. In other words if these problems are normal for adolescents the chances are that the young people will grow out of them and therefore we should intervene only as a last resort. The other view is that we should intervene earlier with relatively minor mental health problems to try to arrest them before they develop into something more serious. As a social worker you need to be clear about where you stand in this respect, as much of our work is at the cross-over point between these views.

Adolescence is a period of development in our lives that is characterised by massive learning and assimilation of ideas as well as having to become a social being learning all the social mores. Writing about adolescence and the life course Crawford and Walker suggest that:

> ... it is the critical process of the development of self, the search for identity and the development of relationships, for example with friends, and the changing nature of relationships, for example with families, that are a central feature of this period of an individual's life.
>
> (Crawford and Walker, 2003, p.70)

It can be an intense time with significant pressures put on young people to perform at school and college and to reach developmental milestones. For some it can be the lack of opportunity and the disinterest of others in them that causes feelings of social exclusion and isolation. At the same time these pressures can produce stress, which as we have seen is one of the key intervening variables in the probable cause of mental health problems and onset of disorder (Chapter 2 provides more detail).

This needs to be put alongside on the one hand the popular view, often seen in the media, that adolescents are becoming more and more troublesome, whilst on the other hand is the romantic view of childhood innocence. Of course neither of these views is totally accurate and they illustrate the ambivalent attitude often shown by adults and the community at large towards adolescents.

RESEARCH SUMMARY

In 1999 the ONS carried out the first nationally representative survey of the mental health of children and adolescents. Results indicate that there are inequalities in children's mental health depending on their household's income. Children from households with lower gross weekly incomes were more likely than those from households with higher incomes to display a mental disorder of some kind. For most income brackets, children aged 11 to 15 were more likely to have a mental disorder than those aged 5 to 10. In addition, children were more likely to suffer from poor mental health if their parents were unemployed, and if their parents had few or no educational qualifications.

Prevalence of mental disorders among children: by gross weekly household income and age of child, 1999: Social Trends, 31

Mental health problems and disorders in children and adolescents

One of the challenges to us is to understand the nature and extent of mental health problems and mental disorder that children and adolescents experience. The Health Advisory

Service (1995) estimated that of the children and adolescent population in the UK the following will at some point experience mental health problems and disorders as below:

2% need the help
of specialist mental
health services

10% exhibit disturbing
behaviours that require
outside advice or help

40% experience occasional
periods of mental distress

Figure 4.1: *Children and Adolescent use of Services in the UK*

These UK statistics can be compared with a 1999 study in the USA that showed that almost 21% of US children and adolescents aged between 9 and 17 had a diagnosable mental health or addictive problem and that for the more serious mental disorder the figure was 11%. The World Health Organisation predicts that there will be a significant increase in psychiatric disorders among children and adolescents that will place such disorders as one of the five most serious causes of death and disability among children (National Institute of Mental Health, 2003).

Good mental health is more than the absence of mental illness and the Mental Health Foundation (1999) suggested that mentally healthy children and adolescents will be those who can:

- develop psychologically, emotionally, creatively, intellectually and physically;

- sustain mutually satisfying relationships with others;

- use and enjoy solitude;

- become aware of others and empathise with them;

- play and learn;

- develop a sense of right and wrong;

- deal with problems and setbacks from time to time.

These development indicators are important for you to understand as they set the context within which you will develop your practice as a social worker, but of course they also require interpretation and reference to any previous history of mental health problems before considering someone's mental health. Equally valid is to get the young person's view of their mental health.

Think back to your childhood and adolescence and using the above list see how well you managed to meet these developmental goals. How many of the above proved at some time in your development to be problematic? What constitutes 'normal' difficulties and what constitutes development that is not normal? Who is it that decides about this? Is it possible that you met the entire list but still had mental health problems?

Of course different people will have had different experiences and some of those will be determined by your gender, ethnicity, family circumstances and, structural reasons like poverty.

Some young people who have experienced mental health problems and disorder believe that these lists do not cover all that is necessary for positive mental health.

Don't lose sight of the reality that it is adults who have determined what is satisfactory or not satisfactory about child and adolescent mental health. Walker points out that there is little evidence of young people having been consulted about their mental health problems. Consequently it is possible that what adults may want from children may well be at odds with what the young people wish for themselves. (Walker, 2003)

Common mental health disorders

Although mental disorder can affect people of all ages there are some aspects that are more usually associated with certain age groups. Some of the more common mental disorders and mental health problems for adolescents are set out below.

Depressive disorders

These include major depression, bipolar and adjustment disorder that adversely affect the mood, energy and general social functioning of the young person. Most adolescents from time to time suffer from mood swings, depression and periods of hyperactivity, but the presence of these depressive disorders is distinguished from these by the duration of the symptoms and the extent that it interferes with everyday life.

There is a growing belief that a small minority of young people show signs of depressive disorders much earlier than has previously been thought and that this may occur during childhood. Depression often affects males and females differently but with both it is often difficult to uncover whether they are unhappy or depressed. The line between this unhappiness, which is short-term, and the longer-term nature of depression is quite difficult to draw. Learning how to do this is down to experience and recognising some of the key signs.

The points at which concerns are raised relate to the extent of the behaviours and their intensity. For instance going into your bedroom for short periods and playing loud music is all part of being an adolescent, but going into your room, locking the door and refusing to have meals or to talk with the family is a point of concern if this lasts more than a few hours. This is a matter of degree and intensity and needs to be compared with previous behaviours.

Depressive disorders are closely associated with an increased risk of suicidal behaviour as the adolescent enters the post-15 years phase. One of the problems that clinicians face in making a diagnosis is that the *Diagnostic and Statistical Manual for Mental Disorders*, one of two psychiatric reference texts, uses criteria that are adult orientated rather than specific to adolescents or children. It is not that these criteria are incorrect but rather that they may be too narrow to cover adolescent behaviour (Pollack, 1999, p.320).

Once a decision has been made to intervene, medication and other talking treatments are indicated and often combined. Both counselling and cognitive behaviour therapy have proved to be effective when working with young people. Medication is often used although this needs to be carefully monitored as much less is known about the effect of this medication on children compared to adults. Indeed some medications, like some of the selective serotonin reuptake inhibitors (SSRIs) which are used extensively with adults, are not licensed for use on people under the age of 18 years as a result of considerable concern about possible side effects.

Hyperkinetic disorders or attention deficit hyperactivity disorder

Hyperkinetic disorder is the term used by British and European physicians when diagnosing attention deficit hyperactivity disorder/attention deficit disorder which it is claimed affects about 4% of the children and adolescents in the USA and a smaller but increasing percentage in the UK, estimated to be about 1%. In part this is as a result of psychiatrists in the UK adopting the more liberal diagnosis that is used in the USA. Signs include impaired functioning in situations where concentration is expected including classrooms and small group meetings. This can also manifest itself with impulsive behaviours and poor levels of functioning in relation to friends.

Interventions can either be medication, often Ritalin, or intensive behaviour modification or in some cases both. Ritalin is a psychostimulant and is from the same family as 'speed'. Although you would expect stimulants to make hyperactive young people more active it does in fact have the opposite effect for most young people.

Stimulant medication works for a short time and has the effect of helping the young person to concentrate and to work better at school as well as at home. Considerable gains in school performance and social ability have been reported. This medication works better when parent(s) are encouraged to provide practical and emotional support for their child. Stimulants are probably overused in the USA and underused in the UK and this medication is prescription only. Unfortunately in the US and increasingly in the UK it is reported that young people sell this medication to their classmates as it also acts as an appetite suppressant. Young people may also 'save up' their medication and take a lot at once to get the 'buzz'. Where stimulants have not worked doctors will often prescribe non-stimulant medication such as imipramine, fluoxetine or clonidine.

Social workers can provide behaviour management, counselling, and psychotherapy. Children and young people will inevitably experience low self-esteem and will be challenging to engage with in any meaningful way. Often parental attention is craved for, even when it is negative, and parents may need your help to learn how to reward positive behaviours and to ignore the negative behaviour. Children with hyperkinetic disorder benefit from being rewarded as much as anyone else even though their extreme behaviour can be especially difficult and demanding. This approach may be as effective as prescribing medication.

It is important that you work with not only the young person and their family but also the school so that everyone is aware of what the intervention is and their role in the treatment plan. Disruptive young people can develop expertise in manipulation and the art of playing off one party against the other.

Dissociative disorders

This condition affects a person's sense of who they are and the extent that they engage with reality. The result can be a feeling of being 'disconnected' from their social world. Everyone can feel this way from time to time; for example long-distance runners sometimes experience a 'high' as they float through a marathon, which could be considered similar. A similar experience can also occur as a result of the side effects of drugs or alcohol.

As you can imagine a diagnosis of dissociative disorder is controversial. However despite this it is likely that this disorder is much more common than previously thought. The diagnosis is often reached only after a series of several earlier misdiagnoses that can include borderline personality disorder and schizophrenia. The most complex of all of the dissociative disorders is known as dissociative identity disorder (DID) or multiple personality disorder in which the person experiences different personalities and often with an overlay of depression, severe mood swings, memory loss, anxiety and panic attacks.

The cause of this range of disorders is unclear but thought to include severe abuse in childhood and the lack of meaningful adult relationships that provide love and comfort. It is almost like the child or adolescent has had to be too self-reliant before they are capable of being so and has forgotten how to switch back to being a child. These disorders are diagnosed using some reliable tools such as the Dissociative Experiences Scale (DES) and the Structured Clinical Interview (SCID-D); a professional who is trained in this assessment tool must administer these. As with all mental disorders the cultural context needs to be uppermost in our minds when making such a diagnosis.

Social workers may work with people who have this disorder by providing information about self-help groups and by working with the person using a range of person-centred approaches. Self-help is often effective as are the various self-help groups and web sites that exist (listed at the end of this chapter).

Self-harm

Self-harm, or self-mutilation, has been estimated to affect as many as one in ten teenagers and is the intentional infliction of harm upon themselves. This can consist of excessive scratching, hitting, banging, biting, pinching or any other form of harming their body. However, most commonly it is cutting or burning themselves. It is important not to misinterpret these actions as suicidal gestures as they imply no intent of suicide (although in extreme cases these actions may result in accidental death).

There is a variety reasons as to why people would do this including self-punishment, to gain feelings of control, clearing their mind, expressing their psychological turmoil physically, seeking attention/manipulating others, and the adrenaline rush that the body naturally releases during these actions. Self-harm, when practised frequently, can escalate and become psychologically as well as physically addictive. The need to experience more severe harm in order to alleviate emotional pain and to attain an adrenaline rush is similar to the way that a heroin addict would use increasing amounts of heroin in order to feel the 'high' they initially felt. Due to this a reliance on self-harm may develop which is difficult to stop. It is important for them to form a new coping strategy to replace this addictive habit.

Eating disorders

Eating disorders involve serious disturbances of the 'normal' eating pattern, and an obsessive concentration on body size and diet. These disorders can be seen on a continuum from minimal intervention in the community through to life threatening conditions that require specialist residential services. Eating disorders are real, treatable mental disorders that can cause considerable distress to those who are experiencing the effects of the disorder and to their carers. (This is used as a case study later in this chapter.)

Social work interventions

Interventions range from working with families to individual work. You need to reflect on some of the value and ethical issues when working with young people. In Chapter 1 the issue of who is the primary client was raised which showed some potential conflicts of interest. In particular the dilemma of conformity with parental demands may be at the expense of the young person's emergent sense of self. Equally, working in an empowering way with the young person may be liberating for them but at the cost of their relationship with their parents and families.

Intervention can take many forms but family support is often the most common and most effective. This can consist of working with the family as a whole and/or working with individuals in the family. The thrust of government policy epitomised in the *Quality Protects* child and family consultation paper (DoH, 1999) is that early intervention by offering advice and support to parents will eventually reduce the number of people who at a young age are diagnosed as having a mental disorder (Walker, 1998).

The choice of intervention is considerable and it is important that services reflect service user needs rather than being resource driven. The following table sets out some of the main interventions that social workers and others might use, depending upon individual circumstances.

Type of intervention	Key aspects
Cognitive behaviour therapy (CBT)	Cognitive techniques challenging negative thoughts and behavioural techniques used to relieve maladaptive thoughts, beliefs and behaviours
Systemic and family therapy	Works on relationships within the family and patterns of interaction between the members
Interpersonal therapy (IPT)	Focuses on the interpersonal relationships of the service user; helps to improve communication patterns and how people relate to one another
Psycho-educational methods	This takes various forms and includes work with service users and families to help them to understand the nature of their disorder and how to promote their mental health
Counselling	Can take many different forms – usually one-to-one and gives the individual the opportunity to develop their understandings of their reactions to events

(Adapted from *Treatment Choice in Psychological Therapies and Counselling*. DoH, 2001)

There are occasions when a combination of interventions works; for example CBT and IPT are effective when working with people who are depressed and help to reduce the symptoms of depression (see above).

With the introduction of Every Child Matters: Change for Children the Government has set out a vision that will if fully enacted see a whole system transformation of children's service. This will be a comprehensive set of changes with the intention clearly set out on the five core ECM documents that set out the strategic planning and the ways in which services need to combine to safeguard vulnerable children. These documents are available on www.everychildmatters.gov.uk.

Of particular interest to you will be the guidance documents that support the effective delivery of services. These include establishing a common core of skills and knowledge, which covers the types of expertise that everyone, not just social workers, needs to possess when working with children, young people and families. It is clear that the government intends to ensure that the various agencies that have contact with children and young people need to work together in new ways to ensure children's services are more effective than at present.

This will include training all professionals who are working in primary care to develop assessment skills to help early identification of issues and emotional problems. The National Service Framework for Children in 2003 restated that children's mental health is everyone's business and set the aim of developing a comprehensive CAMHS service. This will see a rapid growth in training programmes that will try to increase the capacity of the workforce at all levels to be able to cope with these increased expectations.

One of the major features of this approach will be the Common Assessment Framework (CAF), which will be an assessment process that can be used by all the workers in children's services. This is a simplified pre-assessment checklist, a process for carrying out these assessments : a standardised form to record and to share with others. Details of this, including a standard assessment form can be easily found at www.everychildmatters.gov.uk/caf

Consider the following extract from this web site:

> *Training for integrated working will not just be about training staff on specific new processes, it will be one of the most important vehicles for bringing practitioners together, opening up discussions and facilitating change in practice within a local area. In addition, this training must be complementary, and able to be integrated into, the wider Every Child Matters: Change for Children programme and other initatives, especially training on the Common Core of Skills and Knowledge for the Children's Workforce.* (www.everychildmatters.gov.uk/caf)

Services for children and adolescents

Child and Adolescent Mental Health Services are organised into four tiers of service. These are important for professionals who are involved in this area of work to understand as is the connection between the various organisations who provide services for children and adolescents. This structure is set out below and is adapted from the *CAMHS Handbook* (DoH, 1995).

First tier: primary care

This is the level at which interventions are made by GPs, health visitors, school nurses teachers and social workers. The distinguishing feature of this tier is that it is generally provided by non-specialists who can work with children and adolescents in ways that are non-stigmatising but still open up the possibility of early recognition of mental distress. This level of service is usually provided at a local level wherever the professional works.

Second tier

This level of service is provided by a uni-professional group, which includes clinical child psychologists, educational psychologists, child psychiatrists, community child nurses and social workers. This tier offers specialist training for first tier workers and consultation for professionals and their families as well as outreach services where specialist services are not indicated and they also offer assessment for tiers three and four. This level of service is provided at a small number of locations within the community.

Third tier

At this level of service this is a specialist service for people who have more severe and complex disorders. This is typically a multi-disciplinary team often working in a community child mental health clinic or outpatient service. This will include social workers, child and adolescent psychiatrists, clinical psychologists, occupational therapists and art and music therapists.

Fourth tier

This offers access through assessment to child psychiatric services including day units and residential units including in-hospital services for children and adolescents who are in need of highly specialised services. These include services for people who are severely mentally ill or who are at risk of serious self-harm or suicide. These are the most specialised of services and likely to be provided at a supra-region level as not all districts can resource this level of expertise.

Compulsory admission to hospital

For the purposes of the MHA a child is anyone who is under the age of 18 years. There are no lower age limits (other than guardianship, which may not be used for a child under the age of 16 years). Children and young people may be admitted to a psychiatric facility in one of four ways:

1. Informally with their consent providing they are deemed to be 'Gillick competent' – this is a matter for the treating doctor to determine.

2. Informally through the agreement of the parent or someone who has parental responsibility if they are incapable of consent, but note that the 'Deprivation of Liberty Safeguards' under the MCA 2005 do not apply to those under the age of 18 years.

Children who are under 16 but admission would not amount to a deprivation of liberty can be admitted under MCA 2005 ss5 and 6.

3. Under s25 of the Children Act 1989 should be used if the primary reason is to deprive the child or young person of liberty for their own safety or for the safety of others (rather than the treatment of mental disorder).

4. Under the MHA Part 2 or Part 3 would be used if the primary reason is the treatment of mental disorder and they meet other requirements. Note once subject to this order the child could be placed in secure accommodation without a court order becuase this is sufficient power to detain them.

(Fennell, 2007)

The guiding principles are basically the same as for adults, with the note that 'any intervention should be the least restrictive and the least stigmatising option consistent with effective care and treatment but also should result in the least possible separation from family, carer, friends and community or interruption of their education as is consistent with their well-being' (Draft Code of Practice, p212).

Chidren and young people have special needs and it is important that such expertise is mobilised. There is a requirement that at an assessment of a young person, one of the professionals who is involved should be a specialist in CAMHS. This could be an AMHP or a clinician.

If a child or young person is admitted to hospital they should be accommodated in what is referred to as 'age-appropriate facilities', which would exclude admission to an adult ward. This is in fact a limited duty under s131A MHA 1983 to have accommodation that is suitable having regard to his age (subject to his needs).

Children and adolescents who are socially excluded

This group has been identified for specific attention by the government which has set targets for excluding young people and provided funding for specific projects. Such children and young people could be from asylum seeker families, or refugees who may have been witness to considerable trauma, both of which can magnify their experiences of isolation and exclusion in the UK. Although commonsense tells us that such experiences must cause stress and that this can result in mental disorder there is no conclusive evidence. What we do know is that the stress of living in a family at the edges of society is in itself likely to cause mental health problems for members of the family including children. This will include the effects of physical and emotional abuse that may result from continual pressure and the isolation of parents. The impact of racism upon children and such families is under-researched but again it is likely that this is a compounding factor, which results in mental disorder for some young people.

Black and minority ethnic children are, like some of their adult counterparts, over represented in the mental health system. They may have suffered from developmental delay and other problems that are not of their making but may be a result of social exclusions and racism.

ACTIVITY 4.2

Imagine that you are have arranged for a young girl aged 14 to visit you at the office to discuss mental health problems that she has talked about with her teacher. Write down what factors you think are crucial to helping to build up a good relationship with her. e.g. provide a suitable setting.

The ideas that you might have come up with would include:

- *Having a suitable setting that is welcoming, private, safe, secure, has few distractions, materials to draw or write with, comfortable seating alongside each other.*

- *Plan the session and read the previous session's notes.*

- *Boundaries need to be set, identifying what will be discussed and what will not be discussed.*

- *Keeping an open mind is important to allow you to gather valid evidence with the young person acting as your guide.*

- *Listening and reflecting are basic interviewing skills for you to use to get as full a picture as possible about the young person's life and the analysis of their situation.*

- *Empathy and intuition, trying to walk in the young person's shoes, will help you to understand what is going on for the young person and how they assess their situation.*

- *Safety: always ensure that you are not left exposed to allegations about your conduct which may mean that you need to leave the room door open or interview with another colleague.*

(This list is adapted from Walker (2003) pp. 37–8)

Engaging and communicating with adolescents

Adolescents may be referred to you by their parent, teacher, or be seen by you as a result of other work that you are doing with the family. Adolescents are usually difficult to engage in any form of therapeutic work. Many professionals think that specialist mental health services only reach about 20% of adolescents who need these services. For all those adolescents who do reach out and engage there will be many more who will see you once or twice, and that will be enough and they disappear off your files. Of course it could be that even brief interventions can work and it can also be that a positive experience at least sets up the possibility of a return by the adolescent at some later stage.

However it may be important to help adolescents and young people early on in their lives to develop mechanisms that enable them to resolve difficulties that may adversely affect their mental health in later life. If adolescence is a time of transition between life stages it is also a time in which learning occurs about how to deal with the inevitable problems that life throws up. Faulty learning at this stage can result in longer-term mental health problems.

From your experience write down what you think are some of the 'life events' that adolescents may have to deal with when growing up.

We can all draw upon our personal experiences and those of our friends when we went through this stage in our development. Ann Weal (1999) draws upon research to list some of these events which include:

- *conflict in the family;*

- *experience of being in care;*

- *poor development of verbal, literacy and academic skills;*

- *unmet emotional needs.*

To which you probably could have added bullying at school, peer pressure to look good, go to parties, have a boyfriend/girlfriend, have sex, not to have sex, etc. The list quickly grows and with it the potential for tension between competing demands.

Eating disorders

'Eating disorder' is a generic term that includes anorexia nervosa; bulimia and compulsive over-eating. These can develop into serious and often complex disorders that cause considerable anxiety and distress for the young person and their families. MIND estimate that one in 100 women in the UK between the ages of 15 and 30 experiences anorexia. Male representation is much smaller although growing in prevalence. (National Institute of Mental Health, 2001). Eating disorder is ranked as the third most chronic illness in female adolescents (USA brief notes on the mental health of children and adolescents, October 2003).

Anorexia nervosa affects teenagers, usually girls, who are typically perfectionists and have the potential to do well at school. They may have the additional diagnosis of obsessive compulsive disorder (OCD). They will typically have low self-esteem and may believe that they are fat even in the face of seemingly overwhelming evidence that they are emaciated. Many teens experience a fleeting sense of control when refusing food and may enjoy the food battleground that has been created with parents or carers.

Bulimia has different symptoms from anorexia and the teenager will typically binge on huge quantities of food and later eliminate the food through the use of powerful laxatives or self-induced vomiting. Such binges can be alternated with periods of diet. It can be hard for parents and others to discover bulimia as people become quite clever in concealing this condition as the adolescent may be of average weight (due to binging and then dieting). Also purging can occur with any food intake which although strictly would not be classified as bulimia is included as an eating disorder not otherwise specific (EDNOS) or atypical eating disorder.

In diagnostic terms adolescents are usually considered separately from adults as the strict diagnostic criteria of the DSM IV may not be entirely applicable to adolescents. For example adolescence is a time when there is wide variability in weight, height and sexual maturation as well as cognitive development which may make this diagnostic tool unreliable. This can result in some adolescents who have anorexia nervosa going undiagnosed (Society for Adolescent Medicine position paper, 2000.)

The treatment options depend upon the nature and development of the condition. Assessment needs to include clinical manifestations and social and psychological contexts. This is best carried out with an interdisciplinary team approach and may need to cover nutritional advice and counselling.

In a small number of instances there may need to be a period of hospitalisation followed by attendance at a day programme and a supported return to school or the community. The aim should be to provide a seamless transition from inpatient care to outpatient and to be person-centred.

What factors lie behind anorexia and other eating disorders?

A major study involving over 2,000 people in Australia has shown that those who previously dieted to a severe level were five times more likely to experience an eating disorder than those who dieted moderately. This led the research team to suggest that a safer way to control adolescent weight would be through an exercise programme and an educational input about diet and shape.

The connection between diet and the development of eating disorder is not made in every case. However:

> 'every morning hundreds and thousands of women wake up worrying about whether it is going to be a "good day" or a "bad day" in relation to food. They feel remorse for what they ate yesterday and hope that they will have more control today' (Orbach, 1986, p.1).

Orbach suggests that eating disorders, in particular anorexia nervosa, have become metaphors for the way in which society attempts to shape our lives and in this case the bodies of women. In this scenario women find themselves having to mediate their passions and desires, often in a public way, to achieve what they perceive as the desired physical shape. Thus eating can become a ready-made battleground on which women regularly seek to starve themselves to get closer to the perceived perfection of the catwalk model.

While anorexia, bulimia and compulsive overeating do not affect all women, the issues about shape and the centrality of food to the female experience mean that the issues about eating and the realities of eating disorder can be seen as an extreme manifestation of the inner turmoil that many women feel in relation to their bodies. Thus Orbach suggests that the adolescent girl must learn to develop a split between her body and the development of herself and that the girl fantasises over the benefits that might come her way with a slimmer body. This can be hard for men to appreciate and, especially, to understand the messages that men give out to women about their desirability.

There is no overall theory that can explain how this condition begins but there is agreement that stressful events can be seen as an intervening variable that might trigger off mental disorder (see Chapter 2 for a more detailed explanation). However eating disorders are not just about shape and diet, they can occur as the adolescent attempts to get control over their lives. The onset of the condition is sometimes linked to previous sexual abuse or other significant physical or psychological trauma. Another explanation is that it is the unconscious attempt by the young woman to stop her body developing during adolescence. All these ideas are interesting and of course relevant to our study and if you are going to work in this area or experience this condition yourself you will need to read more.

Although there is dispute over the actual cause of eating disorder there are some common factors. The most important of these is the way in which the person needs to feel in control of at least a part of their lives. People with eating disorders often feel that controlling their eating in such a severe manner is the only way that they can control their lives. Those on the outside, paradoxically, may see this as the ultimate expression of someone who has actually lost control of their lives.

This is primarily a condition that affects women, but the number of boys and men affected by eating disorders is on the increase. At present they account for about 10% of identified eating disorders (Neustatter, 2003). It is quite possible that as society becomes more obsessed with the human shape men are beginning to feel the pressure of being the ideal shape and that this striving for the unobtainable perfect body produces casualities on the way.

The social work response

Listening and trying to understand the person's experience and not jumping to conclusions that are not supported by evidence is key. People who experience this distress are often smart, self-critical and competitive people. They can be very able to discuss all aspects of their condition without getting down to the personal reasons about why they are that way and how they can begin to get a better balance in their lives. A review of the literature by Mark Griffith led him to conclude:

> ... and while it might not be possible to offer either an exhaustive nor evidence-based way forward, I think we can say that interventions in general, should be characterised by confidentiality, choice, and a determined effort to engage the adolescent's family. (Griffiths,1998, p.10)

CASE STUDY

Lisa's story

This case study is based on the personal and professional experience of young people who I know and have worked with. I have altered the case to disguise their identities but without losing the essential features. It may surprise you to look at young people's narratives and to see just how many similarities there are between them.

For Lisa the arrival of anorexia was like the arrival of a person who lived inside her head and who had an alternative view of the world. This voice spoke deep down inside and

---

said what to eat and what not to eat. At the age of 14 this voice came to live with Lisa. She couldn't remember the exact day but can recall that the effect was that this voice was struggling for control over her eating habits.

Lisa is a smart young woman who was self-critical and into alternative politics and protests.

At first Lisa was strong and felt that she was able to control the voice and argue with it when the instruction was to eat nothing. The struggle with the voice became very tiring. What do you say to those around you about the arrival of a voice? She was experiencing a degree of dissociation and in particular dissociative identity disorder with each identity assuming control at various times.

The easiest approach was to avoid eating with other people and to have a commitment to a harsh vegetarian diet. These combined made it more acceptable not to eat regular meals. She switched from school meals to a packed lunch, which she threw away. Gradually people around her, her family and friends, began to notice and it became a battleground at meal times. No one understood the struggle that was going on for her with her voice that she thought of as being evil but which no one else knew about. She wore several layers of loose-fitting clothes which hid her weight loss. These strategies concealed the loss of weight and the reality that she had become very skinny.

As Lisa began to lose weight and her skin and hair showed signs of poor nutrition she took the bold step of seeking help from the school and a referral was made to the educational psychologist. At this point she was in a poor frame of mind, worn out by the battles with the voice and lacking in energy. One night she took a large quantity of anti-depressants, paracetamol and anything else that was to hand all washed down with a large quantity of vodka.

Discovered by her mother she was admitted to the accident and emergency unit and given life-saving treatment. The following day she was transferred to a specialist unit. Here she was able to have her eating carefully monitored and to receive specialist input from the team, which included a child and adolescent psychiatrist, psychologist and social worker. She went to a 'group' where she learnt that others had experienced similar situations and also had voices that sought to control their food intake and kept telling them that they were overweight.

The support of the other young people in the unit was especially helpful and contrasted with the general lack of understanding in the world outside of the unit. The unit brought together her immediate family once a week for a Saturday group where attempts were made to help the family recognise the difficulties that Lisa faced and the family's role in this. It was here that the family learnt not to keep on at Lisa for not eating and that trying to persuade her to put on weight was making the situation worse rather than better. It was difficult for the family to accept that Lisa was not doing this to hurt the family but was engaged in a struggle that was hers alone and that the most helpful approach was for them to listen to Lisa, try to understand and to offer their support.

Over a period of a few weeks Lisa got into a position where she pushed the voice into the background and learned some techniques that helped her to keep it there. She was also prescribed anti-depressants and a mood stabiliser from her psychiatrist. Every morning she was weighed and her weight gains recorded. Any loss meant reduction in privileges and closer attention being paid to her diet, a process that she resented but deep down knew helped.

Today Lisa continues to have mental health problems but the eating component of her disorder is at least under control and the eating voice has subsided. Now that she has a more understanding family she can draw some strength from this support although she realises that outside of a small circle there are few people who will understand what she has been through.

Early Intervention

Early warning signs are important to recognise and early intervention may well have prevented Lisa's later hospitalisation. Tiers one and two are usually the first point of service and late referrals can be put down to families and friends mistaking signs of mental health stress as 'natural' or 'normal behaviour' for adolescents. Among the general signs are the following:

Emotional signs

- Sad or anxious without apparent reason and for unusually long periods of time;
- constant concern about appearance;
- feelings of worthlessness.

Behavioural signs

Look for behaviour that has changed recently or causes comment by others:

- poor concentration;
- nightmares/insomnia;
- loss in women of menstrual cycle;
- sudden and unexplained significant weight loss;
- alcohol or drug misuse including laxatives;
- self-induced vomiting;
- concern about diet and calorie counting;
- wants to be alone;
- over-exercising;
- light-headedness and/or fainting;
- evidence of purging.

Recognising early signs

All the above need to be put into the context that change is a 'normal' part of adolescence. Equally, families may be reluctant to seek help fearing the negative effects of labelling of their child. Ignoring early signs of mental health problems in children and young people can have detrimental long-term effects. Early intervention will mean working at the preventative level with young people before their mental health problems become mental disorder.

In Lisa's case several factors were noted as set out below:

- Her parents had divorced and there was still considerable acrimony between them. Lisa was often caught up in the middle of these battles and having to make judgments about competing demands.

- Several friends had noticed that she was more and more withdrawn and spent less time in company and more time on her own listening with headphones to her music.

- She was becoming more obsessive about a number of things including dietary needs, likes and dislikes.

- Her schoolwork had fallen well below her previous level and certainly below what the teachers thought that she was capable of achieving (in some cases there is a sudden dramatic increase in grades).

Tier one services could have helped at this stage and avoided the risk of stigma and labelling that a late referral to the specialist might bring. Increasingly social workers are being located in schools and colleges, which can help mobilise an early response. The Connexions service has Personal Advisors often located in schools who can also provide easy access to services at levels one and two.

ACTIVITY 4.4

You are a social worker placed in a secondary school. Lisa's friends have come to see you as they are concerned about her. What action would you take? Think about this using the 'assessment framework'. Would you:

- *talk to Lisa;*

- *talk to Lisa's parents;*

- *talk to Lisa's teachers and others at the school?*

Depending upon what happened with your preliminary assessment it might be appropriate to refer Lisa for supportive counselling and/or put her in touch with a self-help group. There are also numerous websites that are great sources of information and which Lisa might want to visit. You should check out what your local CAMHS website is.

Interventions

There are two types of interventions, those that are called **psychological therapies** and those that are **clinical interventions** and these are summarised below. Like work with adults the emphasis needs to be on provision of a multi-disciplinary approach that is evidence based. Before using any form of intervention you should check the evidence to see what works best in what situation and what skill level is needed to engage with service users.

Psychotherapy

Psychotherapy focuses upon our inner world and through a process of insight develop-ment, usually on a one to one basis, helps to develop a greater awareness of the nature of an eating disorder and to understand possible causes. Through this understanding people are in a better position to get control over their eating disorder. The theoretical position of this intervention is based in the work of Freud, Klein and Piaget. This form of intervention is usually undertaken by psychologists, psychiatrists or a counsellor and can cover all tiers of CAMHS although usually this intervention is at tiers one and two.

Cognitive behaviour therapy

This focuses not on the inner world of the young person but on the actual behaviours. Here the cause is less important than the manifestation of the behaviours and there is a belief that the causes may not be able to be changed but the behaviours can be altered. The therapist or social worker will work with the person to help them to identify negative and counter-productive thoughts and replace them with a more positive frame of mind. Usually used at tiers one and two.

Psycho-social intervention

This draws upon theoretical positions that are founded in the social sciences and see the person in a social context allowing for intervention that recognises the importance of empowering interventions. Here social workers play a crucial part as they are unique in being able to work with the service user. By so doing they can understand what is happen-ing to the service user and to recognise and intervene to provide access to self-help groups, advocacy, etc. Usually a tiers one and two intervention.

Alternative therapies

These are widely available, often in local community centres or in specialist agencies like MIND, but are increasingly also available for inpatient treatment. These therapies help the person to find alternative ways of expressing themselves through movement, dance, art, poetry and music. There are also a number of self-help texts that some service users report as being very helpful (see further reading). Usually a tier one service but can be across all tiers.

Inpatient

In an extreme case of eating disorder the person's health can be at serious risk as weight loss and nutritional imbalances reach life-threatening proportions. This is tiers three and four and requires a whole-team approach if the condition is to be reversed before long-lasting damage occurs. Specialist clinics are available which may operate under specific therapeutic regimes. Any programme of treatment should form part of a person's agreed care programme (*Code of Practice,* 18, p. 87) and all treatments should follow a full discussion of the form that the treatment will take, and how and when it will be reviewed.

In some cases young people may be 'force fed' under the Mental Health Act (1983) and social workers may be required to sign the legal forms as a person not connected directly with the treatment of the patient but one who knows that patient's circumstances.

Stress busting tips

Managing stressful distractions when trying to study

One of the main problems when trying to get down to serious study is the inner dialogue, which goes on in our minds and keeps playing messages like 'I cannot do this' or 'I am not clever enough' or 'I'd rather do — well anything but this.' Avoidance of hard work like learning seems to be part of a common human condition but using some principles from cognitive therapy can help you to alter these inner conversations and by so doing reduce the impact of stress.

How to turn down the inner voice volume

- Close your eyes.

- Listen to all those negative words until they become clear.

- Imagine this is like a radio – reach out and turn the volume up.

- Listen and make sure that the voices in your head do become louder.

- ENJOY YOUR CONTROL.

- Reach out and turn down the volume – notice how the voices go lower.

- Continue until the sounds become distant and resemble the gentle murmur of the ocean on a still day.

- The sound is still there only now you cannot even make out the words.

- Practise this technique so that managing these internal conversations becomes easier each time that you use this technique.

This method of stress busting requires practice and can be effective for you. With care and skill it can also be used when working with adolescents who are struggling to engage with school.

FURTHER READING

Steven Walker, (2003) *Social Work and Child and Adolescent Mental Health.* Lyme Regis: Russell House.

This is one of the few and certainly the best reads in this area. In this book you will find many of the ideas in this chapter covered in more depth. All chapters are good but Chapter 7 on socially inclusive practice is relevant to this area of work and pulls together the recent government ideas and gives out ideas for a broad ranging practice that works to combat the worst effects of social exclusion.

Grainne Smith *Anorexia and Bulimia in the Family: One Parent's Practical Guide to Recovery* (2004). Chichester: Wiley:

This is a practical guide, written by a parent whose daughter experienced anorexia, and is good reading as it combines practical advice with latest research.

Useful organisations

MIND – The mental health charity that provides a voice for people with mental health distress and disorder. It also has a range of fact sheets and publications that make essential reading for those who want more information about mental health. It also runs a number of supportive workshops and user groups. This could be your first port of call for alternative health care, information and/or support. www.mind.org.uk

WEBSITES

Dissociative disorder

Useful websites include:
www.dissociation.co.uk
A resource for professionals.

www.mosaicminds.org
A website that offers assistance for survivors of childhood trauma and has a particular focus on dissociative disorder.

www.ukssd.org
This is the UK society for the study of dissociation.

Eating disorders

Eating Disorders Association offers help and support for people who experience eating disorder.
Young person's helpline: 01603 765050.
www.edauk.com

Overeaters Anonymous. Although based in Manchester this organisation runs local groups for compulsive overeaters. Tel: 07000 784985.

Pale Reflections is a popular website for adolescents who find the material accurate and informative.
This is a USA site.
www.pale-reflections.com

Association for Dance Movement Therapy. Promotes dance therapy and can provide lists of locally based qualified therapists.
Email enquiries to dance.voice@cableinet.co.uk

The Institute for Optimum Nutrition. Sells books, tapes and videos and can refer callers to nutritionists throughout the country. Tel: 020 8877 9993
Email allion@ion.ac.uk

The Mental Health Act Commission publishes a series of Guidance Notes among which is the technical and detailed Note No. 3 on *Guidance and Treatment of Anorexia Nervosa under the Mental Health Act 1983* which was published in August 1997. Tel: 0115 943 7100

ADD/ADHD Family Support Group UK offers support for families. Tel: 01373 826045

A great website is provided by the Royal College of Psychiatrists – www.rcpsych.ac.uk – which has information sheets that cover many of the topics in this chapter.

YoungMinds, 102–8 Clerkenwell Road, London EC1M 5SA. Tel: 020 7336 8445
www.youngminds.org.uk

National Institute of Mental Health
www.nimh.nih.gov/publicat/eatingdisorder.cfm

National Institute of Mental Health (2001) *Eating disorder: facts about eating disorders and the search for solutions*. A detailed booklet describing symptoms, causes, and treatment, with information on getting help and coping.

Chapter 5

Working with vulnerable people: adults who are short-term service users

> **3.1.3 Values and ethics**
> The moral concepts of rights, responsibility, freedom, authority and power inherent in the practice of social workers as moral and statutory agents.
> **3.1.4 Social work theory**
> Research-based concepts and critical explanations for social work theory.
> The characteristics of practice in a range of community-based and organisational settings including group care, within statutory, voluntary and private sectors.

The liberty of the individual must be thus far limited; he must not make himself a nuisance to other people.
John Stuart Mill (1859)

Introduction

This chapter introduces some of the key concepts and skills that are needed for the social work role in times of short-term acute need. It builds on the learning that has occurred in earlier chapters. The role of the primary care teams is covered and the need for liaison with other professionals in this area is reinforced. Although there are different approaches when working with service users who have chronic as opposed to acute conditions there are also overlaps between the two and today's short-term user could develop into tomorrow's long-term user. To help you to unravel all of this an illustrative example is used throughout based on an older person who experiences depression.

Assessment of people who pose a risk to themselves is a complex and difficult task whether they live in the community or are hospitalised. If they live in the community one of the goals will be to achieve a balance between providing good quality intervention and avoidance of unnecessary risks. Admission to hospital is used as an example to help you to understand when this is necessary.

A case example is used to show how social workers may need to work with a service user who is potentially suicidal. This highlights key areas such as community care and direct payments.

Emphasis is placed in this chapter on assessment for services and the imaginative use of resources. This will cover how social workers can work with providers to provide 24-hour crisis support services.

Policy context

The statistics

Suicide is one of the major causes of death in England, Wales and Scotland and accounts for approximately 15% of all deaths annually although the exact numbers are unclear due in part to the reluctance sometimes of coroners to find a verdict of suicide. This is partly due to the varying criteria but also because of respect for the families. Thus it is quite likely that this figure of 15% is an under-representation of the actual number of suicides. This means that every year about 4,000 people in England, Wales and Scotland kill themselves. In this figure you will find that men outnumber women by about 2:1 and the main concern is for young men in the 15–24 age range and elderly people over the age of 74 (Williams and Morgan, 1994).

National targets

Suicide reduction
The national suicide prevention strategy for England *Our Healthier Nation* (OHN) was launched in 2002 with the clear if ambitious aim of reducing the death rate from suicide by at least a fifth by the year 2010. Suicide rates overall have shown a downward trend since the 1980s and in 1995/6/7 they were estimated to be 9.2 deaths for each 100,000 population and the 2005 figures show that this is now down to 8.6 deaths per 100,000 well on route to acheiving the 7.3 deaths per 100,000 target in 2009/10/11 (NIMHE, 2006).

The Department of Health monitors these targets and the good news is that they are falling slowly and it is likely that targets will be met. It is also important to learn about the circumstances in which people kill themselves and this is also the subject of official investigation.

The Confidential Inquiry
The Department of Health has established a Confidential Inquiry into Homicides and Suicides by Mentally Ill People, to try to identify more precisely the causes of death and the circumstances surrounding death. This Inquiry has been led by the Royal College of Psychiatry and reports will be published from time to time. The first report was in 1996 and described the detailed examination of 240 suicides of which 154 were outpatients. There are numerous findings but among these are that the most common life event before suicide was the breakdown of a marriage or partnership, followed by: bereavement; physical illness and financial problems (adapted from Eldergill, 1998). Relevant to our case example is the finding that over half the people who had committed suicide had contact with the services the week prior to that event.

Workforce
The National Institute for Mental Health England (NIMHE) National Workforce programme has set some priorities for the modern mental health service that includes developing national capacity for work with service users in the community.

By mid 2006 there are the following:

- 343 crisis resolution teams to provide intensive support;
- 262 assertive outreach teams to provide intensive support for difficult to engage service users;
- 109 early intervention teams to carry out assessment and care for service users who are experiencing the first onset of psychosis (adapted from NIMHE Annual Report, 2006).

Workforce developments:

- 500 community mental health 'gateway' workers;
- 700 additional staff to support carers.

By the end of 2006 the aim was that the workforce capacity would be further developed and the shift from doctors to other healthcare professionals, including social workers and the greater involvement of support staff (NIMHE, 2003).

Now we should make the move from policy to application and consider the case of Mr Skeffling (this is his preferred mode of address). This case is used throughout the remainder of this chapter to show how assessment and intervention can be made and what research and statute should inform the kind of decisions that you as the social worker would be making with the service user.

CASE STUDY

Phase one

Mr Skeffling lives with his wife in a remote country village. He is 68 years old and she is 69 and they have lived in the same area for the last 20 years or so. They have two children, both adults, who live in cities some 55 miles away. Mr Skeffling has become depressed and has been prescribed anti-depressants by his GP. Mrs Skeffling returned home after visiting her son for a couple of days to find her husband in a very distressed state. At first she was unsure if he had been drinking heavily but he eventually told her that he had taken a large amount of his medication all at once and washed it down with his favourite whisky. He said that he was 'absolutely fed up with life – it was all too much and he had had enough'. She called her doctor who made arrangements for Mr Skeffling to be admitted informally to the local psychiatric unit.

The admission to hospital was made in order to provide Mr Skeffling with an environment that could respond to the immediate risk and assess the next step. A referral is made to the community mental health team and as the social worker you visit first thing the following morning. By this time Mr Skeffling has settled and is feeling somewhat embarrassed by in his view 'all the fuss about nothing'. He knows that in the last few months he has been very down, isn't very happy with the diagnosis of depression but wants to go back home as soon as possible.

Depression and suicide

How common is mental disorder among older people? Depression in old age is far more common than many people think. Various estimates suggest that as many as 10% of people aged over 65 experience depression that is sufficient to warrant the involvement of professionals (Mental Health Foundation, 2004). More women are affected than men. Other severe forms of mental disorder are also prevalent including of course the organic form known as dementia. When you consider that in England we are experiencing an ageing population the actual number of older people with mental disorder is gradually rising. There are about ten million people of pensionable age in the UK which is over 20% of the population at large. The number of people over 85 has shown a dramatic increase to the point where in 2001 they were 2% of the population or over one million people.

If you work through these figures you will realise that we are talking big numbers and estimates of one million older people experiencing depression are not far short of reality. But can depression be linked to suicide? The obvious answer is yes, but this does need some careful examination before assuming that one necessarily leads to another. First the reality is that the highest suicide rate is found among elderly people and in particular those over 75. This is still the case even though the actual total number of people who successfully kill themselves has begun to fall in recent years.

General practitioners are at the front line when it comes to recognising depression in people. In the case of older people, depression can be overlooked if the GP wrongly thinks that older people are unlikely to be depressed and instead perhaps concentrates on physical problems. Identifying ways of differentiating depression from the effects of older age, which could include sleep disturbance; lowering of activity levels; lower libido and/or greater level of fatigue presents a challenge for practitioners. There are a number of specialist rating scales that help the professional recognise the symptoms of depression and make this task easier and more valid. These include the Geriatric Depression Scale (GDS) (Ulas and Connor, 1999). Like most disorders early recognition usually offers the best chance for good recovery.

Traditionally services are organised in tiers or levels with access to the higher tiers being through the referral system. Primary care is the first tier with services being provided by the GP and other professionals. The general principle is that people's mental health needs should be met at the lowest tier possible and this will involve other agencies such as social services and the voluntary sector.

Social factors

> **CASE STUDY** *continued*
>
> *After a week in hospital Mr Skeffling returns home agreeing to take the anti-depressant medication and to work with the team to develop the care plan into a more comprehensive one. As the social worker you will take on the role of care coordinator/key worker. This includes visiting him at his home.*
>
> *After two interviews with the couple it is becoming clear that their relationship is not especially strong and that Mr Skeffling feels ignored and isolated. Whereas at one time he was a full-time farm worker he is now retired and on a fixed and modest retirement income. His best friend died last year which has left him with a sense of despair.*

What factors contribute to depression? The psycho-social model, suggested in Chapter 2, helps to identify possible factors and for Mr Skeffling in particular the importance of loss to him. His close friend and really only male friend in the last 20 years has been his near neighbour who died seven months ago. The two of them shared an interest in going to the nearby village pub in the neighbour's car and enjoyed the atmosphere and watching live football matches. Mr Skeffling has been once or twice since but felt very isolated and thought that everyone was looking at him. The only time that he gets out is to go shopping in the nearby town which he finds uninteresting.

Although Mr and Mrs Skeffling have been married for a long time they appear to have got bored with each other's company and when together they frequently niggle at each other. He is critical of how his wife spends her time and their money while she complains that he is taking root in front of the television. Whereas his wife has a circle of female friends whom she meets twice a week in the church hall Mr Skeffling doesn't have anyone to talk to or to confide in.

As a further complicating factor Mr Skeffling's car is playing up and will need major repairs or replacing soon. They both say that they cannot afford a new car or to spend a lot on the repair of their present one. Yet without the car they will be unable to go shopping or to make the odd trip to the town. Their children are adults who live quite a distance from them and only get to visit once a month at best and without a car the couple will not be able to go and see them.

CASE STUDY *continued*

The assessment of the situation that the couple find themselves in is starting to take shape. You should now see what factors you have identified as important from the above illustrative example and the notes afterwards.

The importance of loss as a significant factor in the onset of depression will probably be the first that you picked up. In this case it is a double hit as not only did Mr Skeffling lose his activity but also the only person with whom he appeared to have a close, confiding relationship.

Social work and suicide

Not all suicides are associated with mental disorder although the presence of a severe mental disorder increases the risk of suicide. It has been estimated that of the people who do commit suicide 90% experience mental disorder of some type and of these about 30% have expressed clear intent to kill themselves and 25% are psychiatric outpatients. This presents a real challenge to mental health teams. We now need to examine what factors need to be considered in Mr Skeffling's case.

Colin Pritchard describes various ways of estimating suicide risk and uses the Lettieri scale for older men which pinpoints the following key factors:

1. Recent serious loss.

2. Depression.

3. Element of anger or aggression in their behaviour.

4. Refusal to accept help.

5. Previous suicidal or self-harming history.

6. Failure in a major role of their lives.

(Adapted from Pritchard, 1995)

These represent what might be termed 'negative factors' and if you relate this to Mr Skeffling you can see that numbers 1, 2, 4 and 6 are present in varying degrees. This Lettieri scale is one of a number of measuring tools that assist in the prediction of suicide among the population. There are also several self-assessment scales that are in use. They vary in their clinical usefulness and the main use is to aid decision-making but not to replace it.

It is necessary to distinguish between risk of suicide in the short term and risk in the longer term. It has been estimated that about 2% of those who had one attempt will succeed within a year of the first attempt with a particular risk occurring in the first three months (see Butler and Pritchard, 1983). The difficulty that social workers and other clinicians have is assessing just who are the people who fall into this category. This requires a balance between identifying those most likely to be at risk while not intervening unnecessarily with those who are considered to be a lesser risk.

An additional approach is to work with the service user to help identify with them the positive factors or the 'reasons for living'. This approach assumes that the service user will be able, with help, to identify reasons for their life and to be able to put these alongside the more negative attributes. This helps you to work with the service user to identify their strengths or assets rather than only weaknesses or deficits.

ACTIVITY *5.1*

Write down what you would consider to be the reasons for living that would be relevant for you and then write down what you think Mr Skeffling might say and compare the two.

I hope that you found plenty to put down for yourself. I think that Mr Skeffling would struggle a little with this and probably need prompting but he might list:

- hope that life will change;
- love of his family;
- being scared of the act of suicide;
- moral objections about suicide;
- a view that suicide is a sign of weakness.

(Adapted from Linehan, 1985 in Pritchard, 1995)

Working with people who have attempted suicide

The most important contribution that you can make as a social worker is to manage to work alongside your health colleagues to provide a joint approach yet retaining the essential and unique features of social work. A major concern when working with people who have attempted suicide is how or perhaps even if this should be discussed. There are many excellent texts about working with people who are at risk of suicide or serious self-harm.

In our case the psychiatrist at the unit will have carried out an assessment and this will have been discussed at the care planning meeting that will have taken place before discharge took place. The type of questions would include the following:

Questions about the incident itself:

- What was his intent?

- What is the relationship between his depression and this attempt?

- What is the risk at the present of a further attempt?

- What kind of help would he be willing to accept?

CASE STUDY *continued*

Mr Skeffling denies that this was a serious attempt. He has been suffering from mild to moderately severe depression for the last few months but also admitted that he has not been taking his medication regularly. No particular event led to the attempt but he describes it as a build up of events such as the death of his friend and the increased isolation that he feels. He is willing to work with the team to seek ways of improving his life. This would put him in the low risk category.

Questions about the degree of intent

- Was the attempt planned or impulsive?

- Did he know that he would be found soon after the attempt?

- What drugs were taken? How much alcohol was taken? Were there other drugs that were around but not taken?

- Was a suicide note left?

CASE STUDY *continued*

Mr Skeffling's attempt at suicide was not thought through and it appears impulsive. He used his prescription medication as the means of trying to 'end it all' and chose a time when his wife was out but also not long before he knew that she was going to return. No arrangements for following his death, suicide notes, or update of his will, were evident. These put the likelihood of suicide in the low to moderate category.

Assessment of current problems

- Relationship with family members;

- Financial status;

- Social networks, support isolation;

- General health;

- Use of alcohol or drugs.

The above is adapted from a number of guides to assessment (Butler and Pritchard, 1983; Eldergill, 1998; Pritchard, 1995).

CASE STUDY *continued*

Mr Skeffling's relationship with his wife has worsened over the last few years and he has no other person in whom to confide. He is struggling to get by financially and in particular is really anxious about living where they do and being without a car. His wife has a strong network of friends but most of his have either died or left the area. He does drink at home by himself from time to time and when he does it is often to excess. He is not very optimistic about the future. This puts him in the moderate risk category.

The use of such assessment tools should only be undertaken by someone who is skilled and experienced in their application. They are in common use and different clinicians favour different tools. Eldergill has drawn together some of the research findings in this field and some of these are set out below.

Source	Research findings
J.H.J. Bancroft and P. Marsack, *British Journal of Psychiatry* (1977) 131,394	The risk of completed suicide is increased where there is the presence of mental disorder and alcoholism
A.R. Beisser and J.E. Blanchette, *Diseases of the Nervous System* (1961) XXII, 7, 365–9	The risk of another suicide attempt is most common within three months of the first attempt
S. Ganzler, et al., *Life-Threatening Behaviour* (1971) 1, 184–202	A significant link can be made between attempted suicide attempts and social deprivation
N. Kreitman, *Parasuicide* (John Wiley, 1980)	1–2% of people who attempt suicide kill themselves within 12 months

(Adapted from Eldergill, 1998, p.733)

These research findings need to be put alongside other findings such as:

Safer Services, (1991). National Confidential Inquiry into Suicide and Homicide	Half the people who committed suicide had contact with mental health services in the week prior to the event
	At the last contact 85% were assessed as being low risk
Obafunwa and Busuttil, 1994	30% of all suicides are carried out by people who have seen their family doctor less than three weeks before they took their lives
Modestein and Schwarzenbach, 1992	Non-compliance in taking the prescribed medication is an indicator of risk

All research should be treated in a critical manner but also needs to be carefully considered and referred to by professionals. This is how professionals continually develop yet there is evidence that suggests that while medical practitioners may consult the research as a matter of course this is not the case with other professionals such as social workers.

Risk assessment

The evaluation of the above risk factors needs to be undertaken by a clinician who will weigh these up against the research. In the case of Mr Skeffling his behaviour appears to be more of a response to the present situation and discontent with his social isolation and financial situation than total despair with his life. Mrs Skeffling is on paper a viable carer but their relationship is difficult and more likely to be part of the problem rather than the solution. He has only recently seen the doctor for depression and at the time this was assessed as being mild. Since the initial emergency call out Mr Skeffling appears to be less despairing and to have appreciated the opportunity to talk though his worries with someone who is outside of the family.

ACTIVITY **5.2**

Look back at the developing case of Mr Skeffling and jot down what you think are the risk factors. What role could Mrs Skeffling play in the situation?

Policy background

The late 1980s and the 1990s witnessed the move from a policy that was focused upon long-stay hospital care to one that focused upon the provision of services in the community. The closure of large psychiatric hospitals and their community replacements meant that health and social services in many instances had to learn to work together and this is still an ongoing process. This theme ran throughout many government policy documents with suitably aspirational titles like *Building Bridges* (DoH, 1998); *Partnerships in Action* (DoH, 1998); Modernising Social Services (1998); and *Modernising Mental Health Services* (see DoH, 2002).

Care in the community – expanding services to offer choice

The mental health service as it is evolving has the idea of choice as a central and defining feature. By offering service users choice they can be better matched to appropriate services depending upon their need. That present day services are unresponsive, in many instances, to service user need is generally accepted but in order to have choice there would need to be an excess of supply over demand which seriously impacts on service efficiency. Thus services continually come up against the stark financial realities and it has proved difficult for services that are genuinely user-focused to be developed. To offer genuine choice means starting not with what services can be matched but what the service user needs. This requires innovation on the part of service providers and the imagination of those charged with assessment and planning (Onyett, 1992). It also means considerable resources need to be poured into making community care a positive choice that will enhance the lives of vulnerable people.

The key statute relating to care in the community is the National Health Service and Community Care Act 1990 which actually came into being in 1993. This Act has since been supplemented by The Carers (Recognition and Services Act) 1995, which introduced the right for carers to have an assessment of their needs made alongside the service user's assessment. The Community Care (Direct Payments) Act 1996 also enabled local authorities to provide cash for service users to enable them to purchase the kind of services that they want. The later HSCA 2001 made it a duty from April 2003 for local authorities not just to offer direct payments but extended the coverage to include people of any age. However even with all this legislation community care remains patchy and in many instances problematic.

CASE STUDY *continued*

Mr Skeffling has returned home and an assessment has been carried out to determine if he is eligible for community care services. It is quite clear that his wife, who is unable to drive, is unable and unwilling to take responsibility for her husband's well-being. She is very frightened that he might do something silly to himself.

Getting help depends first on having a Community Care Assessment that meets the 'eligibility criteria'. The assessment places service users into one of the following bands: critical, substantial, moderate or low. The assessment is a full one and may take time to organise and carry out but this does not prevent services from being provided or payments made until this occurs. Too often the assessment is about eligibility for existing services and how best they can be packaged to suit the service user instead of working with the service user to identify what would work well for them and a genuine assessment of need. Any assessment ought to look not only at what is missing but also the strengths of the service user and their individual environment.

The criteria that are used may vary slightly from area to area but will include some of the following in order to be put into the critical band:

- significant health problems have developed or will develop;
- inability to carry out vital personal care or domestic routines;
- social support systems and relationships cannot or will not be sustained;
- family and other social roles and responsibilities cannot or will not be undertaken;
- engagement with vital formal support systems is not being maintained;
- serious risk of harm to self or others exists;
- inability to access community facilities.

CASE STUDY *continued*

From what you have read about Mr Skeffling use the above list to check out if he meets any of the criteria and the level of importance to him.

The extent that he meets the above is largely dependent upon how you see the situation. This is an important point for assessments need to conform with equal opportunities which means taking time and approaching the assessment with the service user and others (if appropriate). Work like this needs skill, patience and transparency and the assessment should be signed off by all interested parties.

In the above activity it is likely that he meets all of those criteria but the question is the extent to which these are seen as vital or significant. Allocating assessment to bands is the next step to decide if he is eligible for community care services. In our example Mr Skeffling may just about meet the social services eligibility criteria at least in the short term.

What services can be provided?

Services will be provided to people who are unable to perform one or more basic tasks of daily living where:

a. informal support (Mrs Skeffling) cannot be reasonably expected to provide them;

b. service users (or their carers) are at significant risk without the provision of such services; or

c. services are clearly aimed at increasing independence.

Services will be provided to:

a. meet essential personal, social and educational needs;

b. ensure that service users and/or carers are not left at significant risk;

c. support carers to continue in their caring role;

d. support people to continue living in the community through a programme of rehabilitation.

Most councils have set up a direct payment support service of some sort to help people purchase their own services and to assist them with the legal obligations of employing personal assistants and accounting for the money. The scheme was widely extended in April 2003, which has resulted in a large increase in take up. Local authorities now have a duty to offer direct payments.

Support and self-help

The scheme that came into being is Direct Payments (Community Care (Direct Payments) Act 1996) that allows service users who are disabled, including people who have mental disorder, to receive cash payments in place of services from social services. The intention is that they will support service users who wish to remain independent but the use has been very restricted (Robbins, 2004). This approach was built on the views of what service users want and it was apparent that they wanted:

> ... *Information, help with ordinary living, support with personal growth and development. They want well co-ordinated packages of treatment, and a plan that takes account of their aspirations for the future.*
> (Robbins, pp.2–3)

The Direct Payments scheme offers another alternative that could be very empowering for the service user. When it was originally launched it had age restrictions and close relatives could not be paid. Unsurprisingly take up was low and these restrictions were removed with the HSCA (2001) legislation. The recipient is also responsible for managing and accounting for the money, which in turn most likely will require assistance and/or training.

Check out on the internet what information your local social care provider gives to poten-tial mental health users. Putting in the key words 'direct payments' into a search engine such as Google *will give you lots of information. If you had a mental disorder would you know where to go to get information and once you have the information would you want to have these payments? Although you might be eligible the thought of having to admin-ister money yourself and to keep accurate and verifiable records may in themselves be a deterrent and turn you away from the direct payment solution. Most local authorities have websites for direct payments although these can be out of date.*

Alternatives to traditional hospital based services

Acute and crisis services are designed to respond to a crisis and offer treatment that is less restrictive and less stigmatising than hospitalisation. The development of a range of options, although slow, is happening where government has taken the lead. The present day emphasis on a mixed economy of providers does not in itself produce variety. As smaller community based units proliferate the danger is that what is created is simply smaller hospitals, which are of course less efficient than a larger hospital that is provided by a single provider. The government has increased the level of funding that is available to mental health services to help finance diverse provision.

If you had a blank sheet of paper and funding was assured what alternatives to hospital would you wish to establish? How would you cater for minority mental health needs?

One of the key components in your deliberations about services ought to have been to work out with service users what they want or feel that they need.

Crisis services have become the new policy initiatives as they offer the potential of arrest-ing a difficult situation before it becomes a full-blown emergency and escalates into a hospital admission. Your list could have included:

- crisis intervention teams;
- 24-hour crisis centres that can include short-term residential facilities;
- safe houses that offer less intensive experiences than the crisis centres;
- home treatment services where a multi-disciplinary team can support service users in their own homes;
- 24-hour telephone support;
- specialist services for people from black and minority ethnic communities.

What service users want in a crisis

Most of all what service users want is not to have any more psychiatric emergencies but if they do, they want a service that is responsive to their needs and provides a range of alternatives to hospital admission. Top of the service user list is a feeling of being in control of their own crisis. This included being involved in:

- crisis pre-planning;
- choice of treatments including complementary medicines;
- independent advocates; and
- access to quality information.

They also want to have someone to listen to them and to understand their explanation of what their crisis is about. Listening is an active process and social workers need to be skilled at this process and be prepared to spend time listening to them and not simply using the interview to detect signposts that assist with diagnosis (Golightley, 1985).

Some service users who have experienced a number of crises have developed their own checklist of what to do and what not to do when they are experiencing difficulty. This can include how to respond when they say that they do not want to take their medication when it is apparent that they are in distress. Another example is how to respond to them when they say that they are hearing voices. The point that they make is that making such a list is relatively easy when they are feeling well and upbeat but when they are distressed they recognise that they can lose their sense of what is best for them.

Intervention

The advent of the current legislations was thought to provide the means for an innovative service, which started from where the service user is rather than from what the available resources are. Thus the care co-ordinator should use their imagination to examine the best way of meeting the needs that have been identified in the assessment.

The most likely success will come from a treatment approach that will embrace a combination of anti-depressants and psycho-social support. The results of research suggest that this combination works and is more effective than either psycho-social intervention or medication on their own.[1] The psycho-social intervention could be a form of cognitive behaviour therapy; task-centred work or solution-focused work. This would be in addition to work with the more social aspects such as finances and isolation. With this in mind let us return to our case study and Mr Skeffling (Figure 5.1).

On this visual note the influencing factors have been noted. This could be taken further by the use of dotted lines where the some aspects are weaker than others or by using as above different lengths of line and point. This gives a quick and easy picture of the challenges that are facing Mr Skeffling.

---

[1] See Pritchard, 1995, p.122 for a detailed discussion of the combination of treatments.

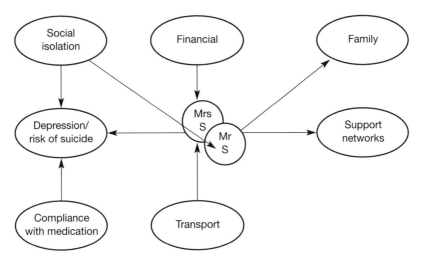

Figure 5.1: *Visual note of the analysis of Mr Skeffling's psycho-social needs*

ACTIVITY **5.5**

Using the visual note try to work out what the team could actually do to make Mr Skeffling feel more happy and more connected to his world. Take each oval and write down two or three tasks or aims. Once you have done this try to prioritise which ones should be tackled first and think about why this is so.

Taking your list you could now put them into categories such as those that stabilise the situation, those that will maintain him at home, those that support the clinical input, those that bring about personal growth and enhance coping skills and those that help to improve his social interaction with his wife.

Needs or wants

One of the long running debates is the choice between what the service user may express as their want and what you and other professionals assess as their needs. Preferences may be expressed for example for a course of psychoanalysis by a service user but the cost of this is so prohibitive that it is seldom funded through the NHS. The allocation of scarce resources will always make some decisions difficult and make the realities of empowerment a challenge for social workers to meet.

Empowerment must remain the aim as well as equal opportunities and anti-oppressive practice. To practise in such a principled manner is also to work in what was called in Chapter 1 a culturally sensitive way. This is also necessary as all decisions are open to greater scrutiny since the enactment of the Human Rights Act 1998. Under s. 47(1) of the NHSCCA 1990 provision is made for the assessment of the need for community care services. This opens up the prospect of service users being unhappy with the assessment because it doesn't meet their wants as it is based on an assessment of a professional's view of their needs.

Mrs Skeffling is unhappy with the services that have been provided for her husband.

Mrs Skeffling can of course complain, as could Mr Skeffling. There is a precise complaints procedure that allows first the complaint to be resolved locally and then if that is not to her satisfaction it can move up the hierarchy. All local authorities and other care providers must show in writing how a complaint can be made. As a social worker you must inform service users and carers of their rights to complain (NHSCCA s.50). She is also entitled to her own assessment of her needs carried out in tandem with the assessment of her husband's (Johns, 2003).

You may want to consider the idea of 'spiritual healing', which has been developed by John Swinton (2001) in his interesting book *Spirituality and Mental Health Care*. Whatever your views might be about the place of spirituality it is the case that for many users and carers spirituality is a very important concept. Swinton puts forward a model of social care that includes a spiritual dimension:

> *Care that takes seriously the spiritual dimensions of human beings requires an approach that draws carers into the deepest, most mysterious realms of human experience and allows them to function empathetically within a context that is often strange and alien.*

> (Swinton, p.136).

The question which he rightly poses is how this approach can be made accessible to people who have mental health problems. The answer if indeed there is a single answer starts with focus being placed on the people themselves rather than on the implications of their diagnosis. This requires using a different approach and asking of the service user 'What gives the service user's life meaning?' And what can be done to enhance their meaning and connectedness?

Swinton suggests that such a basic refocusing enables the professional to see the situation as the service user sees it and to accept as valid the person's concerns rather than seeing the service user as a diagnostic entity. At its best this is a developed and deep communication with the service user. This is close to my ideas of phenomenology (Chapter 2, page 25) which is a way of psychiatrists and others using empathy at the heart of their approach.

Swinton takes this on further by arguing that serious attempts to 'walk in the service user's shoes' means that we need to learn a whole new language and ideas. The term 'interpathy' has been coined to describe the entry into the world of the service user and the genuine way of attempting to understand what they are experiencing. This is more than empathy as it has the extra dimension of exploration of the service user's world.

Social workers have an important part to play in this process as one of the few professionals who can interact with the service user, their families and community. The skills that you have learned and are learning should put you in a good position to be able to help others as well as yourself to understand service users and if you choose to work in this way to help them to find spiritual meaning in their lives.

Providing for individual need

By now you should be able to see that the most effective intervention will be based upon an accurate and negotiated assessment of needs that has been agreed between the service user and the professionals. The actual provision of services will vary depending upon the individual's circumstances and the imagination of the care co-ordinator and of course the assessment of eligibility.

ACTIVITY 5.6

Sketch out what your plan would be and check out the extent to which it meets the visual note.

My plan would be:

- To provide individual work with Mr Skeffling. This could be in the form of cognitive therapy. The aim is to help him to increase his coping skills.

- To provide information for the family about the nature of depression and suicide.

- To ensure that he has a copy of the Charter which gives him information about his rights, including the right to complain.

- To help him consider using direct payments to provide transport to the therapeutic day centre and to see the doctor. He would also like to attend a stress reduction class. To help him to enrol on the nearby history class which will also require daytime transport.

- To encourage him to go the CAB to have a financial makeover as there is a strong possibility that they are under-claiming benefits.

- To provide a short series of couple work to help them to look at their relationship and to respond to some of the anxieties and fears that Mrs Skeffling has which may be manifesting in her attitude towards him.

- To use the local MIND office to identify social support networks and to put him in touch with the local user group. They have older persons' groups and a day centre run by the members for the members. This will provide an easy route to helping Mr Skeffling to develop a network. Maintaining a network is much easier than starting one up from scratch.

- To arrange for a support worker to meet with him and go with him to the shops and get a coffee. This can also be used to encourage him to take his medication. This could be an effective use of direct payments. One of the aims is for him to develop a positive relationship whereby Mr Skeffling feels that he always has someone he can call if he needs to.

- To work with him to encourage and motivate him to want to get better and to do so by continuing to take his medication. As this has been a problem for him in the past this should be high priority.

- To work with Mr Skeffling to help him to write in a diary on a daily basis how he is feeling and what challenges he has faced. This will enable him to look back with his social worker to identify any patterns that might exist and to be able to recognise these and find ways of dealing with them.

- To develop with him a contract as the basis for future work. This will specify mutual expectations as well as what he wants people to do if it is noticed that he is becoming withdrawn or talking about it all being too much. This could also include keeping a diary record of his drinking habits.

- To arrange that he visits the 'crisis centre' and makes some contact with them. Now he is in the system he can access the services there should the need arise and there is a 24-hour help line. There is a short stay residential facility at the centre, which can be accessed through a professional referral.

Monitoring and review

Like all plans they should be regarded as work in progress and subject to modification if and when the situation dictates. The best plans are those that all parties understand and of which they have shared ownership. Mr Skeffling at present is positive and wanting to develop his coping skills and to improve his relationship with his wife. The plan can facilitate this to happen but may need to be modified as people react differently to change.

C H A P T E R S U M M A R Y

In this chapter you have explored working with service users who need services from time to time. The emerging forms of community care, if used imaginatively and with adequate funding, should offer service users improved services. Community care assessment is crucial to this process and in this chapter the example of an older man who is depressed and potentially suicidal has been used to illustrate some of the key points that social workers must understand in order that they can play a central role in the provision of community services.

Imagination and innovation are probably not the first words most people would use to describe the process of assessment and planning but they are essential attributes that need to be a part of the overall empowering approach. Situations like the case study are often complex and to work effectively you will need to understand not just your role but how that fits in with other professionals. You will find it difficult to be empowering of others when you are unsure yourself.

FURTHER READING

Wlliams, R and Gethin Morgan, H. (eds) (1994) *Suicide Prevention: the Challenge confronted: A manual of guidance for the purchasers and providers of mental health care.* NHS Health Service Thematic Reviews. Well worth reading and contains useful checklists and discussion.

Colin Pritchard's book *Suicide – The Ultimate Rejection* contains most of what you need to learn about the psycho-social aspects of working to predict and prevent suicide. It was published in 1995 and although parts are getting a little tired it is heading towards becoming a classic read.

Useful organisations include:

Depression Alliance: www.depressionalliance.org/

MIND: www.mind.org.uk/

National Self-Harm Network: www.nshn.co.uk/

Survivors Speak Out: www.gude-informatom.org.uk

Values into Action at www.viauk.org

Mental Health Foundation: www.mentalhealth.org.uk

Chapter 6

Working with vulnerable people: adults who are long-term service users

A C H I E V I N G   A   S O C I A L   W O R K   D E G R E E

This chapter will help you to meet the following National Occupational Standards.

Key Role 1: Prepare for and work with individuals, families, carers, groups and communities to assess their needs and circumstances

- Assess needs and options to recommend a course of action.

Key Role 2: Plan, carry out, review and evaluate social work practice with individuals, families, carers, groups and communities and other professionals

- Interact with individuals, families, carers, groups and communities to achieve change and development and to improve life opportunities.
- Address behaviour which presents a risk to individuals, families, carers, groups and communities.

Key Role 6: Demonstrate professional competence in social work practice

- Research, analyse, evaluate and use current knowledge of best social work practice.
- Work within agreed standards of social work practice and ensure own professional development.

It will also introduce you to the following academic standards as set out in the subject benchmark statement that includes:

4 Defining principles

4.1 As an applied academic subject, social work is characterised by a distinctive focus on practice in complex social situations to promote and protect individual and collective well-being.

4.3 There are competing views in society at large on the nature of social work and on its place and purpose.

4.6 Social work is a moral activity that requires practitioners to recognise the dignity of the individual, but also to make and implement difficult decisions (including restriction of liberty) in human situations that involve the potential for benefit or harm.

5 Knowledge, understanding and skills

5.1.1 Social work services and service users.

The nature and validity of different definitions of, and explanations for, the characteristics and circumstances of service users and the services required by them.

The relationship between agency policies, legal requirements and professional boundaries in shaping the nature of services provided in inter-disciplinary contexts and the issues associated with working across professional boundaries and within different disciplinary groups.

5.1.2 The service delivery context

The issues and trends in modern public and social policy and their relationship to contemporary practice and service delivery in social work.

The significance of legislative and legal frameworks and service delivery standards (including the nature of legal authority, the application of legislation in practice, statutory accountability and tensions between statute, policy and practice).

The current range and appropriateness of statutory, voluntary and private agencies providing community-based, day-care, residential and other services and the organisational systems inherent within these.

5.1.3 Values and ethics

The moral concepts of rights, responsibility, freedom, authority and power inherent in the practice of social workers as moral and statutory agents.

Introduction

This chapter will help you understand the type of social work that is used when working with long-term and enduring mental health service users. The example of social work with people who have a diagnosis of schizophrenia is used to illustrate various aspects that are important when engaging with long-term service users. This will help you to understand the role that social workers and other professionals play in the treatment of people with schizophrenia. Working with long-term users can be a very demanding task and brings to the fore issues about liberty, dangerousness and the different parts that we all can play in the management of mental disorder.

> It isn't that they can't see the solution. It is that they can't see the problem.
> G.K. Chesterton (1935)

Social work is an applied subject and:

> ... is characterised by a distinctive focus on practice in complex social situations to promote and protect individual and collective well being. At honours degree level the study of social work involves the integrated study of subject specific knowledge, skills and values and the critical application of research knowledge from the social and human sciences (and closely related domains) to inform understanding and to underpin action, reflection and evaluation.
> (Subject benchmark statement)

Nowhere is this more relevant than in working with vulnerable people who have enduring or chronic forms of mental disorder, such as schizophrenia. This chapter will bring together some of the learning that has taken place in previous chapters about values and ethics, legal processes and context and understanding about mental disorder and some of the forms of treatment. Unlike the first four chapters in this book the last three start from the world of practice to give you the opportunity of learning about work with specific mental disorders.

Long-term users who experience schizophrenia

> **CASE STUDY**
>
> *John is a mature student at university who lives with his father and his stepmother in an inner city area. He was admitted to the local psychiatric hospital on Saturday evening following an incident in which the police were involved. The events surrounding the admission are unclear, but it seems that John's stepmother had called the social services duty team when his behaviour became extreme and she felt threatened.*

The initial contact

As a social worker you have picked up this case on Monday morning when you arrived at the office. There is a handwritten report from the duty Approved Social Worker following John's admission to hospital. It appears that he was persuaded to go into hospital on an informal basis and is there now.

Multiethnic society

ACTIVITY 6.1

No mention has been made of whether John was from a minority ethnic group. What assumptions, if any, did you make about this? What difference would it make if John were Afro-Caribbean? Can you recall the impact of mental health in the black and minority ethnic communities?

Effective social work practice is one that is culturally sensitive, appropriate and examines personal, social and structural explanations for mental disorder. However to do this well you need to know about the different impacts that mental disorder has on people and in the case of Afro-Caribbean young men they are much more likely than their white majority equivalents to be admitted compulsorily under the MHA 1983. Figures do vary but one reliable and possibly conservative estimate is that Afro-Caribbean men are three times more likely to be admitted. Some medical practitioners suggest that stigmatisation and racism are likely to account for these differences in admission rates (Bhopal, 1998).

CASE STUDY continued

The next steps taken were to read John's file and to begin to refine an understanding of what had happened. The files make interesting reading and tell the story of a person who has been diagnosed as having paranoid schizophrenia and has been drifting in and out of contact with the services over the last five or so years. There is some evidence that he regularly abuses alcohol and that he likes to use recreational drugs such as cannabis and ecstasy. As a strong man he can present a rather threatening manner to people who annoy him and the previous social worker says that he has a 'short fuse'.

Assessment: the first stage

The gathering of information is an essential part of preparing for effective intervention (see Parker and Bradley, 2003). This process will probably be familiar to you and diagrammatically looks like this.

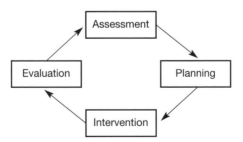

Assessment consists of a number of possibilities. In this case it could include:

- Gathering information from the user's file which helps to paint a picture of the sort of contact that has gone on with this service user and under what circumstances.

- Meeting with the stakeholders – a modernist term that includes the service user and their family or carer.

- Discussion with the other professionals who are involved with the service user.

With this in mind the case file shows that similar incidents have occurred three times over the last couple of years and John has been detained on two of those occasions. He has been in and out of employment and decided this year that he would start at university with a view to a career in the health and social care professions. John has had several social workers including a student social worker over this period and the file has some major gaps. Unfortunately the compilation of records is often treated as low priority by many social workers and it is at times like this that it becomes obvious that this means a certain degree of starting over again. When users have been detained in hospital there is a statutory requirement that a care plan should be completed and that this needs to involve the stakeholders who include John, his father and stepmother. When this has been properly carried out it will provide the full cycle of assessment, planning, intervention and evaluation for work with the service user up to the point that it is considered that the user no longer requires this level of service.

The picture that is emerging is of a young man who has few friends and remains living with his father and stepmother. He has few outside interests and the file shows that the relationships at home are not very supportive.

CASE STUDY *continued*

The visit to the home is quite illuminating as both John's father and his stepmother initially present themselves as well educated, caring people. However as the interview progresses it becomes clear that while they may be caring, they are very critical of John and his social attitude and general behaviour. His father regards it as a failure that he is unable to live up to the brother's example. He went to Cambridge University, lives and works in London and is a bright person with a lot of friends. When his father divorced and remarried John's stepmother thought that John had not got used to the idea of being in a new family and sometimes she felt his behaviour was simply to wreck her relationship with his father.

They both felt that John needed sorting out and that the services repeatedly let them down. They said that he was a danger to others when 'ill' and yet no one seemed to be interested in their view.

Dangerousness: who decides

Care in the community has had consistently bad press since the move to close down many hospitals and to relocate the service in the community. The killing in 1992 of Jonathon Zito by Christopher Clunis at a London underground station caught the public imagination and created a form of moral panic. The linking by the media of dangerousness and mental health has meant that the few incidents that have been reported have left an impression in the public mind that is difficult to erase. The effect of this has been unnecessary fear and also to put mental health professionals in the front line where any mistakes are very public.

The reality is that the thousands of decisions that are made correctly seldom get coverage. For those of you who are football fans the mental health professional is rather like the goalkeeper who makes hundreds of saves and is hardly noticed but if one error is made no one lets him/her forget. This is not to condone poor practice as this needs eradicating where it exists, but in work that is necessarily complex and involves risk management things will not always work out as you predicted.

In spite of the above it is important that we study the cases where things have gone wrong and make sure that we learn from them. Subsequent inquiries have been well reported and in general show a degree of what is called 'system failure' characterised by a breakdown in communication and understanding between the various agencies that are involved. This has in turn resulted in a lack of trust not only by the public in services, but also it seems by government ministers who seem to be ever more influenced by interest groups as well as the impact of adverse publicity. However, this degree of panic reaction has and is being conducted largely in a research vacuum. The reality is that we simply do not know if the public is at an increased level of risk from mentally disordered patients (Coid, 1996).

CASE STUDY

In 2003, 19-year-old Daniel Rogerson was convicted of manslaughter with diminished responsibility after attacking and stabbing to death a 78-year-old neighbour in a sleepy village in Lancashire. In another instance Paul Kahn attacked and killed a complete stranger called Brian Dodd on a North Wales beach. Both of the attackers were people who were known to the services and had a history of severe mental illness. Both had a history of carers having sought help from services and in their opinions they were not responded to in an appropriate way.

However the evidence that is available shows that although the incidences are in reality very low, there are a small number of people who are likely to engage in violent acts. It is evident that people with severe mental disorder who exhibit violent behaviour are much more likely to kill themselves rather than others.

The ability to predict who will carry out such acts is limited and far from a science. With this in mind Coid calls for:

- better training for mental health professionals in assessment and treatment;

- more effective training in risk assessment and management; and

- patients who behave dangerously and default from treatment should not be allowed to become ill in the community.

   (Coid, p.967).

In John's case there was concern about his behaviour, but there was no evidence that he was actually violent. It is important to distinguish between what is verifiable evidence and what is speculation. Among the factors that need to be considered are:

- past history of violence which is the most reliable means of determining future conduct;

- poor compliance with treatment and aftercare;

- substance misuse; and

- recent severe stress.

This stage is still about gathering information about John and trying to determine what this episode means for him and his family. Once you have got about as much information as you are going to get, the next step is to determine what to do with the information.

Involving service users in risk assessment and management

Research commissioned by the Joseph Rowntree Foundation examined the involvement of users in their own risk assessment and management. The work was carried out in England and interviews were in-depth with users, carers and professionals. The findings include:

> Many service users were aware that they could pose a risk to other people when experiencing psychosis and wanted to reduce the chances of this happening.
> Levels of agreement between service users and professionals about risk and how to respond to it ranged from full agreement to very little or none; and serious gaps were sometimes found in information held about service users that potentially put themselves and others at risk.
> (Joseph Rowntree Foundation, April 2004)

This shows that there is a lack of consistency in the overall approach to working with risk and risk management and much depends upon the individual professional. The researchers suggest that there needs to be a format for assessing risk and the subsequent management plan incorporates service users' views (Langan and Lindow, 2004).

The hospital visit

Shortly after the family has been interviewed John is visited on the ward. An initial and brief conversation with the nurse in charge reveals that John is in quite a distressed state and is receiving anti-psychotic medications. He is hearing voices and can exhibit challenging behaviour from time to time. The initial diagnosis has been confirmed as paranoid schizophrenia. This is also an important time for you to discuss with the nurse your safety when meeting with John. It is not the time for bravado as putting yourself in a potentially dangerous position is good for neither you nor John. In this instance the view is that the situation is safe, but as a precaution you are given a waist fitting alarm.

Understanding the impact of schizophrenia

In Chapter 2 some of the characteristics of schizophrenia were described which is information that you would need to know prior to your visit with John to enable you to discuss the treatment and care plan for John with the other professionals. The model that was used in this chapter suggests that even with disorders that have a physiological or genetic component to them stress plays an important part. People with schizophrenia have a high sensitivity to stressful events which can trigger the onset of an episode of schizophrenia. Such events can be located in life events such as divorce or loss of someone close to them, but could also include the loss of work or other events outside of their personal or family domain.

One of the features of some forms of schizophrenia is the experience of auditory hallucinations, commonly known as 'hearing voices'. Some people who have schizophrenia also have feelings of thoughts being inserted into their mind or have visual hallucinations. Interestingly these are usually culturally specific with people in the west hearing voices from space or computers while people from less developed countries may report hearing voices that are more to do with religion or demonic possession.

ACTIVITY **6.2**

Understanding what the arrival of schizophrenia must mean to people is crucial for you as a social worker. We talk about walking in the other person's shoes and you should find whatever source you can in order to do this. You may be fortunate in that on your course there are service users who have had mental health experiences and they might be willing to share these experiences with you.

Understanding visual hallucinations is a feature of the movie A Beautiful Mind *that shows the life of the brilliant professor John Nash who works at an Ivy League University in the USA and has been a lifetime sufferer from schizophrenia that includes visual hallucinations. If possible try to see this film.*

CASE STUDY *continued*

During your interview with John he begins to act rather distanced and when you check with him he tells you that he is hearing voices. This poses a real challenge because you have never come across this before and you are not sure what to do.

Working with people who are hearing voices and experiencing delusions

Katie Glover (2000) has written a very practical guide for communicating with people who have mental health problems and there are some other guides that will help you to understand the best way of working with people who experience delusions or hallucinations.

There are some very practical steps including:

- Recognition that the service user is experiencing voices instead of ignoring them and trying to carry on as if nothing was happening: 'Are you having difficulty following what I am saying?' 'Are you hearing voices?'

- Acknowledge the difficulty and distress that are caused by hearing voices: 'It must be very hard for you to continue with this conversation, thank you for sticking with it.' (Glover, 2000, p.157)

If John has said that it is very distressing you need to acknowledge that you understand and then be prepared to wait for a while or to postpone your interview. What you do not do is be dismissive of John's voices. They are real for him and you are starting from where he is.

Some people experience delusions which means that they are confused about who they are or often where they are. This can be disturbing for the family and disconcerting even for professionals. By and large the work that you would do with people who are deluded is simply a mixture of empathy and honesty. Consequently, faced with someone who says that they are from the secret service you might suggest, 'But now you are in this hospital and I want to work out with you how we can best help you.' This approach acknowledges the presence of the 'delusion' but avoids collusion with it and tries to establish a foothold in reality.

Hospitalisation

John is in hospital on an informal basis which means he can discharge himself at any time, subject to the holding power that is Section 5, MHA 1983, which gives nurses and doctors the right, in certain clearly defined circumstances, to keep John on the ward until a doctor can reassess his condition and evaluate the risks to John or to others (Chapter 3 covers this aspect). He is on an acute admission ward that specialises in the assessment of a patient's disorder and attempts to discharge as soon as possible. John is known to the services, consequently the assessment will not be to determine if he has schizophrenia, but to try to stabilise his current situation to the point where John can return home and a community treatment plan can be agreed between the stakeholders.

As we have seen in Chapter 3 informal patients can refuse treatment in line with common law. This right to refuse can be mediated if the patient is assessed as not having the capacity to make such decisions. Questions around capacity or lack of capacity are ones that medical practitioners have to address, often consulting with other professionals.

John is reasonably content to take his medication which the RMO has prescribed and which includes anti-psychotic medication. This follows, you have learnt, a typical pattern for John. He will take his medication when in hospital and for a short while after discharge back to the community but he then stops his medication or becomes erratic in his self-administration. Changing this into a more reliable pattern becomes one of the goals for his treatment in the community.

CASE STUDY *continued*

John has responded well to treatment and after ten days is already being considered for the next step of returning to the community. You have made more visits to the family and to John on the hospital ward.

If John had been detained on a section of the Mental Health Act 1983 the staff would be obliged to ensure that John was given specific information as soon as practicable about his admission and other information including rights about treatment, detention, renewal and discharge (s.132). This is considered to be good practice and similar information should be made available to John as an informal patient.

Life on the ward is a return to the familiar for John, but even so his experiences have not been overwhelmingly positive. This fits with evaluations of many service users who report concerns about:

- feelings of being unsafe on the ward;

- lack of meaningful activities to keep them occupied;

- insufficient information about their disorder and expectations of the ward staff;

- low levels of one-to-one interaction with the professional staff; and

- lack of involvement with planning their treatment and return to the community.

(See DoH *Mental Health Implementation Guide*, 2002)

Many service users report the importance to them of one or two individuals with whom they had made a significant relationship or the importance of the other service users who helped them to get through the difficulties that they were in. But others feel that they were largely ignored and saw the RMO insufficiently for it to be a major factor in their recovery.

Substance abuse has also emerged as a problem on many acute admissions wards. Staff have to be vigilant to prevent the use of recreational drugs such as crack cocaine on the ward. This not only confuses the treatment regime of patients but can have an impact on the life of the ward in general and other patients in particular. Dual diagnosis is the term used to describe the coexistence of mental disorder with another diagnosis. This can be mental disorder and learning disability or mental disorder and substance abuse. In some inner city areas as many as three patients in ten have a dual diagnosis involving substance abuse with the consequence that they spend longer in hospital than do single diagnosis patients and are up to four times more likely to commit acts of violence than those with the single diagnosis of schizophrenia (*Rethink Sane*, Zito Trust, 2003).

These challenges pose real problems for hospital staff and striking the balance between the need for formal observation, and vigilance against drug dealers can result in a mass of rules and procedures, the net effect of which can make living on a ward more like being in a custodial institution rather than a hospital. Service users need to be listened to and engaged wherever possible in the running of the ward and their care.

Planning for successful intervention: working across agencies

The Care Programme Approach (CPA) has meant that the planning for John's discharge has already got underway and an initial plan has been developed in conjunction with John and using information from the family. This is put alongside the diagnosis, the previous notes and the views of the medical practitioner and the nursing team.

Working across agencies and between professionals from different disciplines has long presented a challenge for professionals who are trying to deliver a community based service that is effective. The introduction by the government of the National Service Framework and the Care Programme Approach (CPA) in 1991 were just two of the features of the new modernised mental health service. The government had a clear idea that the CPA would be the system that ensures that service users would be supported in the community and that this would reduce the chance of them drifting out of contact with the services. The CPA is now to be refocused to essentially have only one layer (instead of the present two) that will refocus effort and resources on the more serious cases which will include all of those patients who have been detained compulsorily. The CPA should produce a holistic service that is co-ordinated and uses a key worker or care coordinator system that takes the lead in all aspects of the involvement with the service user (more detail is provided in Chapter 3).

One of the key aspects of this is an assumed common vision of how the service might work. In one study all the professionals thought that they had clear objectives and a commitment to involving service users. Central to this is the attitude of the workers who are involved and the few evaluations of this tend to show that among nurses, social workers and support workers there is a shared view and a desire to change practices to be more user-focused (Carpenter et al., 2003). However implementation of these modernised services across the country is patchy and research carried out by the NHS Executive and the Social Services Inspectorate in 1997 confirmed that a seamless service that was user-focused and not resource driven, was still an ideal in many parts of the country that was waiting to be implemented (Bartlett and Sandlands, 2003).

The introduction of the National Service Framework (NSFMH) in 1999 set out seven specific standards for providers of services to meet and these included a range of services from community outreach to secure hospitals. The standards apply across the board to both health and social service providers, and standards four and five refer explicitly to inter-agency work and the importance of multi-disciplinary assessment. There is also enabling legislation in the form of the Health Act 1999 that enables local authorities and health authorities to transfer funds to each other in order to promote a seamless service and to generally improve the quality of the service.

When teams come together this creates a common approach, but it would be a mistake to think that this means that everyone has an equal say. In particular, according to anecdotal evidence, doctors and psychiatrists, are ostensibly happy to be a part of the multi-disciplinary team, but only when they retain, to use an American football analogy, the quarterback position (the star position). When this is put alongside research it shows, not surprisingly, the acquiescence of the service user to medical practitioners. Low (2004) writes that what is missing is the concept of active interest and involvement of lay people or, in our terms, service users. The effect of this is to create a new hierarchy in which the service user still remains at the bottom, the professionals, other than doctors, are in agreement with each other while doctors are still on top.

Service users on top

It was the recognition that service users needed to be at the centre of reforms that led the government to embark on a comprehensive listening process to enable the service user voice to be heard. The listening exercise, 'Your health, your care, your say', allowed the public to speak directly to ministers, health professionals, and each other on how improvements could be made to their local services. Included in the 143,000 contributions were many mental health service users and carers. This exercise resulted in July 2005 in the publication of a new White Paper.

The White Paper: *Our health, our care, our say: a new direction for community services*

This Paper recognises how NHS and social care services work together and how these services could adapt to provide individuals with the health and social care services they need closer to their homes The White Paper, *Our health, our care, our say: a new direction for community services*, aims to:

- *change the way these services are provided in communities and make them as flexible as possible;*
- *provide a more personal service that is tailored to the specific health or social care needs of individuals ;*
- *give patients and service users more control over the treatment they receive;*
- *work with health and social care professionals and services to get the most appropriate treatment or care for their needs.*

(DoH *White Paper: Our health, our care, our say: a new direction for community services*, January, 2006)

To achieve these aims will require that all agencies learn to work better together and that service users and carers will have more say in the type of service that they wish for and need. This will give greater emphasis to ideas of partnership – something that training and educational courses will need to remember.

To keep up fully with all the changes that are being proposed there is no better place than to go to the DoH website and to click onto the White Paper Bulletin www.doh.gov.uk/ourhealthourcareoursay

As far as John is concerned you are lucky to be working for one of the newly formed community mental health teams, and it is in this context that you are trying to plan with John a course of treatment and care that will help him to stabilise while in the hospital and eventually to make the important move into the community. Assertive Outreach teams are something of a new invention and in reality it is too early to pass judgement about their effectiveness.

ACTIVITY **6.3**

Think about the realities of working together in one multi-disciplinary team and the notion that service users and workers are in acquiescence to medical practitioners. Is this a good thing? To what extent do you think that this is inevitable? What impact will this have on you if you are to work in a multi-disciplinary team?

Even after recovery from an acute phase, most patients struggle to reintegrate into the community. In John's case, there were few community links prior to hospitalisation so the task of reintegration is even more difficult. Where home life is difficult the importance of work and outside activities increases and part of your task may be to identify what is available in the community. This could include sheltered workshops, day centres, hostel or user groups. A good supportive environment is often to be found at voluntary organisations like MIND, the mental health charity, or other active mental health groups.

Had John been detained on a treatment order (s.37,s.3 etc.) there is a duty on primary care trusts or health authorities and social services departments to provide, in co-operation with the voluntary and independent sector, aftercare services until they are satisfied that the user no longer needs this service. This has caused some local problems as the duty is placed on the area which the user goes to on discharge. This has resulted in some arguments between authorities as to who is responsible and a ruling from the High Court that it is the area from which the patient came when admitted that bears the financial responsibility, with the exception of people who are of no fixed abode (Bartlett and Sandland, 2003).

ACTIVITY 6.4

If John lived in your area what resources would be available for him? It would be helpful to you if you could spend a little time looking around at just what is available. If you have a local MIND *shop they usually have a list of the resources that are in your area and sometimes community mental health teams have similar information.*

Early intervention

The frequent contact with services interspersed with periods of low or no contact is sometimes also referred to as the 'revolving door' and presents a challenge to services. These patterns seem to be entrenched for John, which is unfortunate as research suggests that a key determinant in a person's career as a mental health patient is the speedy and effective response to the initial episode (Frangou and Bryne, 2000).

The first episode, like it was in John's case, happens usually in the late teenage years or early twenties and probably like John the behaviour can go undetected for several months or even longer. This is largely because of the contextual factors that include:

- erratic behaviour that is also a characteristic of late teenage years;
- the known use of recreational drugs like cannabis which confuse the symptoms of psychosis;
- the first signs may be negative ones such as withdrawal, social isolation, and emotional flattening, none of which on their own may cause significant concern; and
- people who hear voices are often reluctant to tell people of this partly because they feel that people will think of them as being mad!

Trigger events

The model used in Chapter 2 helps to conceptualise about the onset and some of the factors that can result in mental disorder such as schizophrenia. Whether the occurrence of an episode is as a result of some event which effectively triggers this, or whether it is inside the person is unclear. However the likelihood is that it is as a result of key events that produce considerable stress for the user.

With the above in mind can you speculate what the triggers might be in John's case? Think of those that might be personal for John and those that are more social.

Trigger events could be the result of some 'unresolved' issue for John, which has left him conflicted; this might be something hugely significant like emotional or other abuse whilst growing up. It could also be as a result of a stressful event that he has been unable to resolve, this could be starting at university and not being able to make social contacts, exacerbated by living at home. It might also be a combination of these.

Although the lifetime prevalence of schizophrenia is about 1% which may seem low to you, the impact of schizophrenia brings with it huge social and personal costs. People who are diagnosed with this severe disorder literally join another tribe and can become isolated. The impact of the disability can be understood in the same way that Oliver (1996) writes about the social model of disability. The disorder itself can have a significant impact upon the person and their families but this is magnified by the association in the public's mind with dangerousness and the difficulties that the public has in dealing with unusual and unpredictable behaviour.

Consequently it really is in everyone's interest that early recognition is made and an appropriate response is made. The use of medication in the first episode is reported as being more likely to succeed as in the initial phase the user may be more responsive to treatment (Frangou and Bryne, 2000). This can take the edge off the psychotic symptoms and be an effective maintenance tool but on its own is probably insufficient.

The prognosis for people diagnosed with schizophrenia is that about 80% will recover but over 70% will have a second episode within a five to seven year period (Frangou and Bryne, 2000). This suggests that treatment should be considered longer term than the initial episode and that long-term courses of antipsychotic medication may be advised. However the most likely successful recovery or maintenance is to be found when the medication is a part of the overall treatment plan and a more holistic approach is used. This fits in with the model that was covered in Chapter 2 that brought together the different components that may impact on and lead to a mental disorder such as schizophrenia.

Although the dominant paradigm is medical the evidence that supports the primacy of a uni-directional approach is hard to find. As a social worker you need to guard against this approach being the only one that you will work with as it brings with it some consequences for the service user and can make your role a secondary one. The advantages of using a more holistic assessment and modelling approach are that you can begin to understand why more Afro-Caribbean young men are diagnosed with schizophrenia than their equivalent white male counterparts. It also helps you to understand the role that families can play in the onset of schizophrenia and, importantly, in the treatment.

Intervention

It is generally considered that family circumstances are important determinants of future success or relapse with people who have schizophrenia. The research shows that relapse is more likely for users who have a diagnosis of schizophrenia if, after a period of hospitalisation, they return to a family that is overly critical or is emotionally over involved and controlling (Brown, in Butler and Pritchard, 1983, p.90). This resulted in the development of a concept called **expressed emotion** (EE), and the rather surprising finding that users may fare better in the community if they do not return to their families.

More recently Pharoah, Mari and Steiner (2000) conducted an evaluation of the effectiveness of family interventions for people with schizophrenia in line with the drive towards increasing the evidence base for various interventions. This evaluation took Brown's work as the starting point for their evaluation and has produced strong evidence that confirmed their work. Even so the use of this approach in a practice setting is limited and it has by and large been left to one or two researchers to 'promote' this approach. The work of Leff, Kuipers and Lam (2002) is an example of this approach being slowly spread to other practitioners (nurses and social workers) through the Thorn Initiative.[1]

Expressed emotion is a clinical concept and the presence of high expressed emotion has a high predictive value. EE is actually a research technique and measures things like critical comments, hostility and over involvement that in turn produce emotions of various strengths. Experiencing high EE can cause considerable stress for some people and, it seems, especially for people with schizophrenia. Work with families involves trying to get families to move from expressing the negative side of emotions to developing techniques and mechanisms that demonstrate the positive aspect of emotion.

Measuring expressed emotion can be carried out using a standardised assessment schedule using the Camberwell Family Interview (CFI) that was developed in the 1960s. This is usually completed by the user's family and because the person has been admitted to hospital the completion of the schedule occurs soon thereafter. Interviews are usually taped and then subject to analysis or scoring over three dimensions which are:

- **criticism** which is measured by scoring the number of overtly critical and specific comments that have been made;

- **hostility** which is scored when there is rejection of the patient as a person or a combination of general criticism and rejection;

- **over involvement** which includes exaggerated emotional responses, usually self-sacrifice and overly devoted behaviour, over protection that is inappropriate to the patient's age, and difficulties in maintaining boundaries.

This requires practice and training as the tone and content of the interview are also taken as measures of the expressed emotion.

[1] The Thorn Initiative is an extensive course in psycho-education approaches pioneered by the Maudsley NHS Trust and the University of Manchester

The treatment model as expressed by Leff et al. (2002) is underpinned by a view that can be summarised as follows:

- schizophrenia has a biological basis but people who are diagnosed are particularly sensitive to stressful events which makes them vulnerable to relapse;

- family members need to join in with therapeutic work as they are both affected by the arrival of schizophrenia and may have contributed unwittingly to the relapse and possible onset;

- honesty, openness and clear communication are important in order to share information about the nature of the disorder and to recognise the limitations of this knowledge;

- families have positive as well as negative features and it is important to build on the strengths; and

- this form of work needs to be carried out together with other forms of intervention and supervision.

As you can see, this is, in reality, a psycho-social education form of intervention in which your role as a social worker is to play the role of educator with the family. While social workers need to be aware of the medical side of mental disorder it is important that they retain their own skill base and capacity to work in an empowering way. This approach is empowering as the family is encouraged to learn more about schizophrenia and to work with the therapists to determine their own solutions to the problems as they see them.

Evidence is being gathered from other countries which shows similar results to that achieved in the UK. Kalfi and Torabi (1996) carried out a study in Iran that included a cross-cultural comparison. This revealed that expressed emotion is an important factor in predicting relapse among users who have schizophrenia who lived in Iran. In a similar vein studies about the impact of high EE in families that contain a user with bipolar disorder or unipolar disorder also look promising.

While to become fully competent in this type of intervention does require additional training the general principles of these approaches can be usefully applied to many situations. As a social worker you could be the champion of an approach that is empowering of the service user while retaining the treatment ethos of a uni-directional approach. This approach encapsulates social factors such as unemployment, substance misuse, poor social networks, and high expressed emotions and puts them alongside the diagnosis of mental disorder as equal partners rather than as subsidiary parts (Tew, 2002).

Working with John and his parents in a holistic manner puts them centre stage and offers them the opportunity to learn about schizophrenia and to understand the effect that their communication patterns may have upon John. In some cases it may be advisable for John to leave his parents' home and to live in other accommodation and 'manage' his relationship with his parents in this way. This enables him to escape the 'trapping' patterns of communication but also does not place the blame for his disorder on the parents. After all, it is very unlikely that parents consciously choose to relate to their children in ways that create problems.

Caring for the carers

Carers of people with long-term mental health use may find the process challenging and debilitating. Those carers who provide regular and substantial care for a person on CPA are covered by Standard Six of the National Service Framework, which to be met, would mean that they receive their own written care plan following discussions with them and your assessment of their physical and mental health needs. This needs to be carried out annually at least.

Assertive Outreach

Assertive Outreach teams are a part of the reform to mental health services in the community. They work in an intensive manner with long-term users of mental health services who are considered to be difficult to engage in treatment. John would probably fall into this category given his history of non-compliance with medication and his readmissions to hospital.

The Sainsbury Centre, in 2003, reviewed the people skills that are needed to work with the typical service user who receives Assertive Outreach. They came up with a list of personal and professional attributes that included being able to:

- work with service users in informal settings;

- work with service users and families in an accepting and certainly uncritical manner;

- hold realistic expectations of service users and the scope for complete recovery; and

- relate to service users' experiences of mental health, possibly through their own experience of oppression or of mental health.

    (Sainsbury Centre, 1998)

The same document also describes some of the evidence that underpins the assertive outreach approach and claims that they can reach a large percentage of hard-to-engage service users and that they are generally liked by service users and their carers. When these teams work well they provide an integrated service that consists of a variety of professional groups including community psychiatric nurses and social workers.

ACTIVITY 6.6

Make some enquiries, if you do not already know, whether there is an Assertive Outreach team in the area in which you live. If they do exist get their information for service users which should help you to understand more about this specialised multi-disciplinary service.

The plan

Your work with John will be informed by your own understanding of the challenges that he faces and your assessment of the trigger events. This is nearly always achieving a balance between what the service user wants, what you and other professionals think that the service user needs and the reality of what is actually available. The process should begin early and have the service user at the front of the deliberations about treatment options. The CPA assumes that the care plan will be drawn tighter with the active involvement of the service user and that they will have agreed and signed the action plan.

With John the plan could take on a number of different shapes and at this point with the little information that you have you should make some notes of three possible plans.

Your three plans would of course be drawn up following discussion with other professionals, John and his family. They might include (but not be limited to) these.

Plan one

Do nothing and let John leave hospital and return home taking antipsychotic medication. They have your telephone number and if the situation worsens they can contact you. The justification for this is that it's the least invasive plan and of course uses the least direct resources. This assumes that you have all decided that John is not a risk to either himself or to others.

Plan two

John returns home taking antipsychotic medication, and with the offer of family work to reduce the level of expressed emotion in the family and with your support he will eventually return to university.

Plan three

John moves to supported living accommodation in town, his family are offered ten sessions to help them to understand how they can change some of their behaviours to help his recovery, he starts going to the local MIND day centre and takes part in a support group run by service users for people hearing voices. The local Assertive Outreach team offers him a package of comprehensive services including monitoring his medication.

CHAPTER SUMMARY

Several themes should be evident in this chapter, not least of which is working in partnership with service users. Because of the debilitating nature of schizophrenia and the low level of public knowledge about the condition you will have to move at a slow pace and be acting as both a therapist and a psycho-social educator. The use of a holistic assessment and psycho-social methods of working is likely to be the most effective social work intervention with people who have long-term schizophrenia (like John).

As a social worker you have a crucial role to play in holistic assessment and in order to fulfil this role you need to be a professionally competent worker who has sufficient knowledge to be able to hold your own with medical practitioners without unnecessary acquiescence to them. Your work should be characterised by empowerment and a high level of specific knowledge about the resources that you have available in your area and about what works.

Priebe and Slade's (2002) book *Evidence in Mental Health Care* (Hove: Brunner-Routledge) has some very useful chapters about what works and with whom. See the chapter on the user perspective about what counts as evidence.

For help and advice about benefits consult *The Big Book of Benefits and Mental Health* from Neath Mind, 32 Victoria Gardens, Neath, SA11 3BH. A ten-page proforma is available online from www.rightsnet.orguk/pdfs/AA

Subject benchmark statements are best accessed through the Quality Assurance Agency (QAA) website: www.QAA.ac.uk and then into subject benchmarks.

Joseph Rowntree Foundation, York: www.jrf.org.uk

Chapter 7
Working across organisational and professional boundaries

The current range and appropriateness of statutory, voluntary and private agencies providing community-based, day-care, residential and other services and the organisational systems inherent within these.

5.1.3 Values and ethics

The moral concepts of rights, responsibility, freedom, authority and power inherent in the practice of social workers as moral and statutory agents.

5.1.4 Social work theory

Research-based concepts and critical explanations for social work theory.

The characteristics of practice in a range of community-based and organisational settings including group care within statutory, voluntary and private sectors.

Introduction

Sunlight is the most powerful of disinfectants and electric light the best policeman.
Mr Justice Brandis (1914)

This final chapter brings together some of the themes from earlier chapters under the heading of working together to provide an integrated service that is efficient and effective. Providing an integrated service that will protect children is used as an example although the need to work together applies across the whole range of services. The links with other chapters, such as Chapter 4 on child and adolescent services, will be all too apparent but in this chapter the primary focus is upon providing the service user with a needs-led service that does not involve them having to be referred to other agencies.

Children are rightly the focus of this chapter because they may be in need of mental health services because of individual mental disorder; they may be being parented by someone who is themselves experiencing mental disorder or they could be the unfortunate subject of a fabricated mental disorder. In the UK 2–5% of children are brought by their carers to the attention of Primary Care Teams with mental health issues as the main presenting problem. It is likely that many more children with mental health problems do not present at all (Spender et al., 2001).

At the extreme end the pressing issue of child protection and mental health is explored using the Victoria Climbié Inquiry and others as examples of the need to put children first, irrespective of different professional boundaries. The Green Paper *Every Child Matters* (September, 2003) focuses on the support that parents and carers should have; early intervention and effective protection; issues of accountability and integration regionally and nationally and the need for workforce reform.

Every Child Matters: Next steps was published in March 2004 and set out the ways in which the proposals in the Green Paper could be enacted. At the same time legislation was introduced in the form of the Children Act 2004 to set out a new national service framework for children whilst retaining the 1989 Children Act.

Community-based services have now become one of the dominant organisational forms from which mental health services are provided and this chapter will help students to understand the roles that they can perform in such services. These will include working as a 'care co-ordinator' to provide direct services and as an 'assessment officer' to determine the extent that services should and can be provided.

Evidence-based practice is introduced to point you to the ways that the professions will progress.

Working with service users as individuals and with service user action groups has become a standard way of working but one that requires considerable skill and understanding, both of which are explored as an aid to student learning.

Service users' views

A more recent development of these ideas is termed 'The Circle of Involvement ' which is a simple way of understanding how it is necessary and what steps need to be taken to ensure that service users become more involved. This was conceived out of work that was carried out in the Trent region and brings together key components such as education and training, government policies, service development and workforce development. By visualising these components as a circle that is seamless and that one component feeds in to the other it is possible to work towards greater involvement at any stage (*Principles for Practice*, December 2005).

Involving service users owes its origins to the Children Act and the 1990 NHS and Community Care Act, both of which placed the involvement of service users on the agenda. The idea of citizen participation goes back much further than this and can be traced to town planning and the work of Sheri Arnstein (1969) who first developed a 'ladder of participation' and subsequently to the community social work and community development movements of the 1970s. This has gained considerable momentum with the requirement put onto social work courses to involve service users in all aspects of social work training. Where this is taken seriously it will undoubtedly be a transformatory process and could result in major changes to education and training. However it is still too early to evaluate if the involvement of service users will be more than just a fine idea.

The mental health service user movement includes those that are involved at the governmental level such as MIND and YoungMinds, both of which regularly submit high quality detailed analyses to inform policy making. There are also examples of patient controlled services such as Camden Mind and the influential Patient Councils. In addition there are local user groups which may be affiliated to the national bodies such as SANE or MIND or Survivors Speak Out and specialist groups such as Women in Special Hospitals.

Service users of course need to be consulted about the services that they receive to help find out what sort of intervention works well and why. However, in contrast with clinical drugs trials, all too often the evaluations that have been carried out are about satisfaction with the services received when what is desperately needed is an evaluation of what worked and the extent to which it worked.

Service users can be involved at different levels:

- individual level where they work with the professionals to determine what is the most appropriate way of responding to their mental health needs;
- group level with service users working together, with or without professional facilitation, to support each other;

- activist groups where they comment upon aspects of service delivery and challenge or inform conventional operational practices;
- involvement at a strategic level to plan services or training courses such as service user groups or as individual representatives;
- involvement in national bodies to campaign for changes and to offer government policy-makers advice and assistance.

The involvement of service users varies according to what level they want to become involved at and what is available. At each level there is also the prospect that within that level will be specialist interests such as black and minority ethnic or women's groups. The key for social workers is to form alliances with service user groups and to work with them in ways that will recognise the contribution that both can make in moving towards a mental health service that is user-focused and emancipatory.

ACTIVITY **7.1**

Some organisations work as pressure groups campaigning for what they see as necessary changes to mental health law and services. Now is the time for you to go onto the internet and check out at least one of these sites. The YoungMinds website www.youngminds.org.uk is usually one of the best for a wide range of coverage of mental health issues.

The involvement of adult service users has been slow to get underway and at times somewhat tokenistic. However there has been progress with even less children and adolescent involvement. It is surprising given the legislation about children's rights that they can be so easily overlooked and the adult view of what children want dominates. Even the present proposals to reform the legislation state that when considering individual treatment for children and young people the clinical team must consider the wishes and feelings of the child while they must take *'proper account'* of the parental view. This took into account the view that children may not be competent to determine their own treatment but this is seemingly contradictory with the Richardson Committee suggestion that children should be considered competent from the age of 10 –12 and that competence should be assessed according to the Gillick judgement.

ACTIVITY **7.2**

What reasons can you come up with to explain why the perspectives of children and young people have not been considered in respect of mental health services? How valid is this? Would lowering the age at which people can vote to 16 make any difference?

The Equality Act 2006

The Equality Act received Royal Assent on 16 February 2006. This legislation will bring about some major changes and may well provide impetus to the greater involvement of people with mental health problems in mainstream service delivery. The first part of the Act effectively sets up a replacement body for the Equal Opportunities Commission (EOC), the Commission for Racial Equality (CRE), and Disability Rights Commission (DRC). The new body is to be called the Commission for Equality and Human Rights (CEHR) and will promote equality irrespective of age, religious belief, gender, and sexual orientation and will come into being October 2007. The second part of the Act will extend protection against discrimination and provide protection for people against discrimination on the grounds that they have no religious belief.

Working towards an integrated service

The idea of working together to provide a seamless service to service users is far from new. In 1976 as a part of a research team we published my first major piece of mental health research (Jones et al., 1985). This was a project led by Professor Kathleen Jones of York University and was a tracer study to examine the destinations of nearly 200 patients who had been discharged from York psychiatric hospitals over a two-year period. In that research we examined the ways that agencies tried to work together or to be more frank the ways that they didn't manage to work together! Back then we talked about agencies 'collaborating' a rather strange term given that collaboration means working with the enemy! Since then I have followed with personal and professional interest how things have moved on and it is timely to revisit the idea about working together.

Integrated services are services that are joined together to provide one access route for service users. Such services imply common training to at least some extent and shared values. Multi-disciplinary approaches retain the professional and often organisational identity of the professional involved.

Multi-disciplinary teams

The multi-disciplinary team exists both as a community mental health team, and in a form that includes professionals who work in the team part-time and also work back in their own agencies. A child mental health team could comprise members as in Figure 7.1, although this will vary from agency to agency. The first point for involvement will usually be a referral from the family doctor to this team for assessment, and if intervention is planned a care co-ordinator will be appointed who will carry the responsibility for the case. This can be the scene for some power struggles between the professions and also within the professions. General practitioners are often more comfortable dealing with another medical colleague than relating to a different professional. Consultants will point out that they have clinical responsibility for the individual and hence medical–legal responsibility. This has been further compounded with the emergence of nurse prescribers. These issues can be sorted out and it is important that the multi-disciplinary team establishes clear operating procedures.

Figure 7.1 *Child mental health team*

The emergence of a new, planned workforce

The National Workforce Action Team was established to determine what the demand for staff might be and what type of staff was needed for the modernised mental health service. Poor workforce planning has resulted in much of the present services developing in an ad hoc way that reflects more circumstance, history and influence than effective planning. The slowness of establishing joint planning teams has hindered the development of widespread effective integrated services. The Workforce Action Team pointed out that poor planning was in part the result of the limited links that agencies had with each other and the general lack of enthusiasm across professions to implement flexible working practices and cooperation (Alcock, 2003).

One of the exciting developments in community mental health has been to recognise the importance of factors such as community support and networking. This is important work, which can make a huge difference to the experience of the service user. This has coincided with the emergence of a new support worker with a new type of qualification. These roles are close to those of social work but are more limited in their scope. Some professionals see this new form of worker as a threat to their role and simply a means by which government can cut the wage bill. What do you think?

The management of mental health professionals

Careful risk assessment is necessary for any person who is engaged in direct work with people who are under the age of 18 years and are provided with health or social care services, especially in the light of the Allitt Inquiry (see later in this chapter). This includes health screening to ensure that they are fit for employment and that any condition which is revealed can be managed in a way that will not adversely affect their work with service users or colleagues. This is a balancing act that requires careful assessment, especially in the light of the need to reduce discrimination that people with disabilities, including mental disorder, experience.

The list of Inquiries that permeate social work makes monumental reading but there are valuable lessons that must be learnt if the profession is to progress and vulnerable people be better served. It is to these that we briefly turn.

Learning from Inquiries

Two Inquiries are described, the most recent concerning the circumstances around the death of Victoria Climbié and the other that of the nurse Beverley Allitt who was convicted of the murder of several children at the hospital ward where she worked. They are but two of many, far too many, Inquiries into the untimely death of people who in different ways had expected the services to have done more to protect them. Although each Inquiry has some specific lessons that need to be learned, together they point out that some of the basics that make up competent practice have not been taken on board.

The Victoria Climbié case

Victoria was a healthy, lively, happy young girl who had been sent to England by her mother in the hope that she would be well educated and achieve her potential. What parent would not want this for their child? However this was not to be and in the space of a few months she was tortured, humiliated and in the end died. At the post-mortem examination she had over 128 separate injuries all over her body. In the final few weeks of her life social workers made attempts to see Victoria but made the incorrect assumption that she and her carer had moved. That the result was tragic is self-evident but that it could have been prevented is a shocking indictment of professional services including social workers (Johns, 2003).

Were Victoria's carers mentally disordered or just sadistic people? There certainly is an argument that can be made to support the view that anyone who tortures and kills a person must be mentally disordered even though in this case the sentencing suggests that this was not an argument that found favour with the jury.

What lessons can be learned?

1. Social workers and other professionals should learn to listen to children and not to dismiss what they say. This needs to be put alongside observations that add to the child's explanation.

2. Social workers should be clear about the purpose of contact with service users and what information needs to be gathered to clarify levels of accountability (recommendation 5, Climbié).

3. Staffing levels, training and management all are in need of improvement and monitoring.

4. As far as mental health services are concerned the following has emerged:

- more support for young carers is needed;

- the overall approach should be multi-disciplinary with a lead professional involved; and

- there should be a common assessment framework.

The Child and Adolescent Services (CAMHS) received additional funding to develop a more comprehensive approach to child mental health problems (see Chapter 4). In addition to these measures the various bodies charged with monitoring compliance with national standards are asking social services and trusts to provide information about the arrangements for safeguarding children and to ensure that their staff are suitably trained and aware of their responsibilities towards children.

Example of Sure Start work: Parenting Matters

Parenting Matters is a course that is run in numerous parts of the country. It is a 30-hour programme held over 12 days to help parents share experiences, remember their own childhood, develop listening skills and learn how to set clear boundaries. Early evaluation shows increases in self-esteem and reduction in authoritarian attitudes. (Parenting Plus; Sure Start, 2004)

The Allitt Inquiry

In the early part of 1991 three children died suddenly and unexpectedly on the children's ward at Grantham and Kesteven General Hospital. There were further 'emergencies' later that year which finally aroused suspicion and a police investigation started. The suspicion was that someone was deliberately harming children on the ward. Eventually this was traced to a young nurse called Beverley Allitt who was subsequently charged with four murders, nine attempted murders and nine accounts of causing grievous bodily harm. While on duty in the children's ward in her local hospital, she tried to kill at least 23 children by injecting them with insulin and potassium, choking, breaking ribs and asphyxiation.

Beverley Allitt suffered from the rare Munchausen's Syndrome by Proxy which is a variation of Munchausen's Syndrome, in which individuals fake symptoms or harm themselves so that they can be the centre of attention. The syndrome is named after a German soldier renowned for telling exaggerated stories. There is still no convincing theory about the causes of this disorder and it is quite rare. Beverly Allitt was sentenced to 13 life sentences and was transferred to a high security psychiatric unit.

Sir Cecil Clothier conducted the Inquiry that followed in 1994. Among many findings was the following comment:

> *Taken in isolation, these fragments of medical evidence were not all very significant nor was the failure to recognise some of them very culpable. But collectively they would have amounted to an unmistakable portrait of malevolence. The principal failure of those concerned lay in not collecting together those pieces of evidence.*
> (Clothier, 1994, p.131)

There are concerns that over-vigilance may result in spurious identification of false risk, a topic which resulted in widespread discussion, including in the House of Lords where the possibility of such a condition being widespread was considered and the possibility of false diagnosis discussed (Lords Hansard, 1997).

> *Put at its simplest, there is all the difference in the world between a Beverley Allitt, whose severe personality disorder led her to murder young children, and a mother who invents reasons why she and her child should visit the doctor. Yet under the all-embracing banner of MSBP, and in the hands of the untrained, the two are treated as being practically indistinguishable. It does not matter whether one calls the condition MSBP or factitious illness by proxy, or by any other name. The point remains the same.*
> (Lords Hansard, 1997)

What lessons can be learned?

The Allitt Inquiry demonstrated four aspects that are particularly relevant for this chapter:

- The need to look out for patterns that help to explain what otherwise might look to be phenomena that are unconnected. This means keeping an open mind and discussing your ideas with others.

- The need to establish and operate a strong whistleblowing protocol that allows other professionals to raise concerns about questionable practice and for these to be followed up.

- The importance of staff screening, and regular supervision and monitoring of performance.

- The professional culture should be underpinned by values and driven by the empowering practice that is open to challenge.

In light of these Inquiries we need to ask ourselves just how we protect children who are at risk and promote their positive mental health and ability to cope with adverse and stressful situations.

Child protection

The policy and legal context

The main legislation is the Children Act 1989 which applies to a person under the age of 18 and the Mental Health Act 1983. Various provisions in the Children Act permit the psychiatric examination of a child although once the child is of sufficient understanding, using the Gillick rules, the child can refuse to be examined (Eldergill, 1997). If the court decides that there is a chance of significant harm a Child Assessment Order (s.43 Children Act 1989) can be made that authorises a child assessment including a psychiatric assessment. There are additional powers available to the courts that include the making of an interim care order and care order. Harm includes impairment of health, which includes mental health (s.31 (9) Children Act 1989). This is important as the community care legislation in general does not apply to children or only applies in a qualified way. (For a more detailed explanation of the relevant law in this area see Chapters 3 and 4 in Robert John's *Using the Law in Social Work,* 2005, in this series).

It is important to realise that although considerable attention goes to the relatively small number of children who are at risk of being or who have actually been seriously abused, a much greater number of children have their development seriously challenged by adverse events, many of which are outside of their control or influence. These need to be considered by social workers and others.

In 1998 the government published a Green Paper called *Supporting Families*, which made clear that the government's mission was 'to put children first'. This was an important statement at a time in the UK when the divorce and separation rate is rising and children can be the innocent victims of these separations. The changed circumstances of parents can mean reduced income levels, changes to school, meeting new 'step-parents' and much more. The policy is to support parents and children undergoing these changes through a wide variety of initiatives.

The publication in 2003 of another Green Paper *Every Child Matters*, which followed the tragic death of Victoria Climbié, called for the strengthening of existing services to provide a universal and non-stigmatising service that children and young people could access through the education system, as well as the creation of new and more focused services for those children who needed additional support.

New duties were imposed on local authorities and what is termed their relevant partners under section 10 of the Children Act 2004. This is an enabling piece of legislation designed to be a key driver in the Government plans to provide more comprehensive service for children. Included in these is the duty on local authorities and partners to co-operate to improve children's well being.

Well-being is defined in the five outcomes for children to:

- Be healthy
- Be safe
- Enjoy and achieve
- Make a positive contribution and
- Achieve economic well being.

The speed of the changes is fast and the extent of the impact probably little appreciated by those who are not directly involved. Fortunately the relevant website permits close and detailed scrutiny and some free downloads of key documents is permitted.

One of the changes will be how services are organised and key to these is the establishment in most areas of Children's Trust that will take the lead role in the coordination of local health, social care and education services as well as other agencies such as Sure Start that may be working with children. This raises all sorts of issues about governance and even in some areas issues about geographical boundaries. The majority of areas will have had to have a Children's and Young People's Plan in operation by April 2006 which will set out in an accessible format the strategic direction the area will take to safeguard children.

The workforce capacity to respond to this initiative is crucial and we know that large numbers of people who work with children are presently unqualified and most likely underskilled (DoH Core Standards, 2004).

This is a high level of integration, which will mean many agencies will have to rethink how they can engage in collaborative processes. Among the children who have been identified as requiring a high degree of integrated services are those who have 'special circumstances' which includes looked after children; children of parents who experience mental health problems and children who are exposed to domestic violence and family breakdown.

One of the key parts of the new integrated service has been the design and trialing of what is known as the Common Assessment Framework (CAF). This is a standardised approach to the assessment of a young person's needs and should provide early indication of the requirement for services. This is an holistic assessment that includes the role of parents, carers and the impact of external factors such as environment. As this is such a cornerstone of *Every Child Matters* most areas have seen a comprehensive rollout programme being established. All forms are available on the web and are in downloadable word format so you can familiarise yourself with this assessment tool (www.everychildmatters.gov.uk/resources-and-practice).

So far we have examined Inquiries to learn about when things go wrong and how the government is making a huge investment that should promote children and young people's life chances.

Does the separation of parents adversely affect the mental health of their children?

It is estimated that at least one in three children will experience parental separation before they reach the age of 16. Should this trend continue this would need to be looked on as the norm for families and we need to recognise that children need to learn coping skills that will better equip them to cope with these transitions. The research commissioned by JRF shows that no matter how well handled these separations might be they are difficult for children and young people to cope with. Although most will experience this as a period of unhappiness and distress that they work through, there are others who will struggle to cope with the effects that this has had on their lives. A small minority will experience mental health problems and some will need specialist help. In *Foundations* (2004) *Together and Apart* the JRF research shows among other highlights that the following are relevant:

- the quality of the parental relationship is important for the child's successful adjustment to post-separation circumstances;
- the older the child the more difficult it is to adjust to being in a stepfamily;
- extended families can play an important supportive role at the time of separation;
- at the time of separation the child's interests can be overlooked as a consequence of the preoccupation of the parental need;
- different children want different services, some like these to be at school and others want services that are outside of school.

However children whose parents separate can benefit from the separation if it is handled well and it is much healthier to grow up in a reconstituted family that is at peace with each other than to remain in a family whose parents are continually at war with each other.

Connexions have developed differently in different areas but you should have found that they offer a one-stop high street drop-in facility. Personal advisors are often located in local schools and again can provide career guidance as well as personal and group coun-selling. This can provide a stigma-free valuable support service for young people as well as an early warning of problems. They refer young people on to other professions when it is clear to them that the person's needs are greater than they can provide for.

Problems that occur in the first few years

The risk of depression in mothers after childbirth (postpartum period) is greater than at any other time, with at least one woman in ten having a depressive episode within 12 months and the risk is greatest in the first three months after childbirth (Spender et al., 2001). Depression among adults has been covered in earlier chapters and we need to con-sider the impact on the child where the mother is distracted from the usual childrearing to deal with her own problems.

The cause of depression in mothers most likely has a biological component to it as does having a history of mental disorder, but once again social factors such as isolation, unem-ployment, lack of a confiding relationship, lack of supporting social networks are all factors that are likely to increase the risk of depression occurring. Childbirth is a major life event, mostly full of joy but also an event that requires a considerable change in lifestyle of the parent(s).

The impact on a mother and partner, if there is one, can be considerable and signs that would usually be picked up as possible indicators of depression can often be dismissed as simply the impact of a new baby. Depression needs to be distinguished from the onset of 'baby blues', which is very common and usually occurs in the first ten days but then goes, and depression, the onset of which is much later. There are numerous scales, such as the Edinburgh Postnatal Screening Depression Scale, that can be used to assess for depression. Health visitors and general practitioners should always be alert to this possibility, not least of which is being aware of the risk to the child in this situation.

RESEARCH EXAMPLE

In a programme developed with the Sainsbury Centre for Mental Health in Edinburgh, Staffordshire and Lewisham health visitors were trained to use a post-natal questionnaire and problem-solving skills. The impact of this training was evaluated using random con-trol trials and the results suggest that the intervention was at least as effective as the use of anti-depressant medication (Sure Start, 2004).

Sure Start projects

We can get a good look at where government policy is going with the Sure Start programme that aims to rectify some of the consequences of social exclusion and inequalities and in so doing to achieve better outcomes for children, parents and communities by:

- increasing the availability of childcare for all children;
- improving health, education and emotional development for young children;
- supporting parents as parents and in their aspirations towards employment.

There are now 524 Sure Start projects across the country both in inner city and rural areas and the government is aiming to open 1,700 centres by 2008. The centres have been introduced to help tackle child poverty by improving children's social and educational development and helping parents balance work and family life. They are trying in locally determined ways to work in disadvantaged areas to influence service delivery as well as to provide direct services themselves. The work is evaluated both at local and national level and early indications are positive that these projects are making a difference.

While adult community health teams focus almost exclusively on the effect on the adult of severe and enduring mental illness, Sure Start programmes focus on depression in adults, mainly mothers, and the effect this had on their children's emotional development. The involvement of Sure Start programmes in the CAMHS programmes also varied, often dependent on the networks and background of the co-ordinator. Some projects had CAMHS workers seconded to them on a part-term basis, others were used to provide the 'user perspective'. What most of the Sure Start projects wanted was to help bring about changes in mental health services to move away from a reactive clinic style approach to a more proactive community-based style of working. Services need to be accessible and at the same time offer privacy and confidentiality (YoungMinds, Sure Start, Conference 2003).

The innovative approach used by Sure Start to develop positive mental health is seen by them as integral to their overall approach. They have targeted key factors for intervention and influence and have created very attractive placement and work settings for social workers. Sure Start have established crèches, parent circles and parent education groups, all of which have the effect of helping develop awareness of the importance of promoting resilience and emotional health among parents and children. There is a long way to go but the impact of these initiatives ought to be significant in the long term.

Problems that occur in school age children

There are numerous behavioural problems that might beset some school age children. One of the difficult tasks is being able to differentiate between what in the present day is considered to be unruly or unusual behaviour and when that becomes a source of genuine concern as an indication of mental disorder. Not least of these is the somewhat controversial presence of attention deficit hyperactive disorder covered in Chapter 4.

Children whose parents have mental disorders

The effect on children who have at least one parent with a mental disorder is worthy of consideration. If we go back to the importance of stress as an intervening variable it is possible to realise the impact that mental disorder of a parent can have on the child caught in this situation. A study of 100 reviews of child deaths where abuse and neglect were factors showed that parental mental disorder was present in one third of these cases (*Red Manual Code of Practice*, 2004).

Research carried out in the Netherlands examined the available literature and gathered together a panel of mental health practitioners all of whom had direct practice experience of working with children and their families (Rikken, 1995). They sought to identify what needed to be present to promote positive mental health. Out of this research came a number of findings including:

- the seriousness and chronicity of the parent's disorder was a significant factor;
- the quality of the relationship between the parent with mental disorder and the remaining parent was significant;
- the age and resilience of the child was an important variable; and
- the nature and extent of the social network to support the family.

The intervention in the Dutch project centred on work with the child and the 'healthy' parent, work to educate the family about the nature of the disorder and the development of social support networks. This is supported by other research showing that community-orientated and proactive initiatives are delivering measurable improvements in parenting skills (Davis and Spur, 1998; Hutchings et al., 1998; Walker, 2003).

Chapter 2 pulled together various factors that put people at risk of developing mental disorder. The impact on the children whose parents have mental disorder was described as being: problems at school, isolation and lack of specific information about their parent's mental disorder and prognosis. The outcome for children whose parent has a mental disorder will vary according to the severity of some of the variables mentioned earlier and will also depend upon the resilience and coping abilities of the child. However if a child grows up in a household where one of their parents has a chronic mental disorder they are at a greater risk of developing mental health problems than if their parent did not have a mental disorder.

This is considered to be so important that YoungMinds have suggested to the government that whenever an adult is diagnosed as experiencing a mental disorder, the law should require that the psychiatrist determines if that adult has parental responsibility for a child and if so that the psychiatrist has a duty to inform social services. This would allow extra support to be given to the family and child to mitigate against some of the negative factors surrounding their parent's mental disorder.

Of course there are other factors that can seriously disturb child development, such as having carers who abuse drugs, something that is becoming more and more common.

Safeguarding children in whom illness is fabricated or induced

A Department of Health Guidance document for Area Child Protection Committees recognised that children may be at risk as a result of their carer attempting to have them diagnosed with some form of illness. Here we see played out a familiar tension referred to by the earlier information from the Lords Hansard about how to protect children from real but rare events, while not wrongly accusing carers of deliberate attempts to harm the children in their care.

There are four main ways that the carer may fabricate or induce illness in a child. These include:

• signs and symptoms;

• falsification of medical records;

• falsification of bodily fluids and/or letters or records; and

• induction of illness by different means.

(adapted from DoH, 2001)

It is important to realise that while as a social worker you should be aware of this phenomenon and alert when vulnerable people are at risk, the diagnosis of this disorder needs to be left with specialists who are experienced and have training in this type of diagnosis.

Understanding children

Sally Gorin at the NSPCC has carried out a literature review that draws together evidence about how children have experienced living with domestic violence, parental substance abuse and parental ill health, both physical and mental. This can make some children very vulnerable and in need of support. The themes that emerged included:

• children are much more aware of their parent's problems than the parents imagined which in turn can lead to high levels of concern about their parent's safety;

• children tend to use informal support and talk to either parents, siblings or friends;

• when they did go to professionals they were not always satisfied with their contact and felt that they were not listened to, whereas what they wanted was someone to listen to them and in whom they could place their trust;

• age-appropriate information was needed to help children to understand what is going on in their family.

(Adapted from Gorin in *Findings*, 2004 JRF)

The following gives a good picture of what the experience must be like and how children feel.

> *Sadness and isolation that children may experience can be perpetuated by the stigma and secrecy that surrounds domestic violence, parental substance misuse and ill health. Some children report feeling depressed, having problems making or maintaining friends, having a disrupted education or experiencing bullying.*
> (*Findings*, May 2004, p.2)

149

Not all children suffer long-term effects and they are often very resilient and bounce back from these adverse conditions.

Assessment of risk and resilience

It is commonly thought that when children are exposed to adverse and stressful situations their mental health will suffer. This is in spite of evidence that suggests that there is not a causal relationship. Clearly in a relatively small number of instances children are at immediate risk of serious harm and the numerous Inquiries where this was overlooked make sobering reading. However it is also the case that many, many more children experience turmoil and adversity in their lives and not only survive it but actually do well. Is it possible that in concentrating upon the individual risk, for all the right reasons, we might overlook the positive effect that social factors might make to help the individuals cope with adversity? Have we got the balance right between protecting children from risk and promoting in them the ability to bounce back when they experience difficulties? Certain key factors crop up time and time again when we look at how some people experience distress and cope. These are described by the term resilience.

Resilience has a near-universal meaning to it and is best summed up as:

> Resilient children are better equipped to resist stress and adversity, cope with change and uncertainty, and to recover faster and more completely from traumatic events or episodes. (Newman and Blackburn, 2001, p.1)

There is extensive documentation of both risk and resilience in the social science and social work literature (Rutter, 1999; Walker, 2003) and the common factors that can be deduced fit well into the schematic chart that was presented in Chapter 2. If we take the main headings used in the chart we can list the following factors.

Social causation factors
- Having a strong extended family;
- successful schooling;
- network of friends
- having a role outside of the family – volunteering, sports, clubs;
- member of a religious community.

Psychological factors
- Warm, supportive carers;
- good parent–child relationships;
- parental harmony;
- confiding relationship with at least one parent.

Personal

- Age;

- higher IQ;

- social skills;

- humour;

- temperament.

(Adapted from Newman and Blackburn, 2002)

However where the above are not present and replaced by low income/poverty, over-involved parents and social exclusion then the child's ability to bounce back from adverse and stressful events is much less likely to occur. Although as social workers we are often involved in short-term crisis resolution, the most damaging impact on child development is most likely to be where the situation is chronic and with little prospect of improvement.

A psycho-social educational approach with parents

ACTIVITY *7.4*

What strategies could be adopted in order to help children to cope better and develop resilience? Write down what you think could be done and by whom. Spend a few minutes on this task.

It ought to help if you refer to Figure 2.1 that was used in Chapter 2. This will give you direct clues about where the need might be but this tool is better at analysis rather than strategy. What works for children coping with adverse situations is having the support of their extended family, neighbours or mentors and having close friends in whom to confide, rather than the specific activities of professionals. (Newman and Blackburn, 2002). How different was this to your ideas? Should the social work task be one of mobilising community support, supporting, befriending and building up a data base for service users to make contact with each other? Children need to have opportunities to learn coping skills in the face of difficult situations. They need to develop self-esteem and to feel valued if not at home then outside of the home. Social workers and others should always look to the strengths as well as the problems in each individual's situation.

Empowering intervention

The psycho-social model of intervention provides a conceptual tool for social workers to work with the diverse populations that make up the UK.

ACTIVITY **7.5**

As a social worker working with Asian children you realise that they are trying to respond to their parents' cultural practices when at home and to the cultural norms of their white friends when at school. As they are getting older the tension between the two is becoming more apparent and their behaviour at school is becoming a problem. The teachers at the local school have asked you to give some advice to them. What would be your response?

Of course there is no easy answer. The use of the psychosocial model allows you to conceptualise some of the problems and to see them as potentially having an adverse impact on the children's development. You are trying to work anti-oppressively but just who is your client? What cultural norms would you respect?

Evidence-based practice

How do we know what works, why it works and with whom it works best? These questions should be at the heart of the reflective practitioner and throughout this book an attempt has been made to locate practice alongside evidence. If social work is to stand alongside other professions we must be able to support our claim with evidence that what we do actually works.

There are a number of information systems that provide up-to-date research reports about mental health and other work with service users. Facilities such as the Cochrane Library, The NHS Centre for Reviews and Dissemination and the newly created Social Care Institute for Excellence (SCIE) will provide academics and practitioners with electronic forms of data and research evaluations. But this on its own it is insufficient and social workers will need to take advantage of the new social work curriculum to enhance their own evaluative and research skills in order to make best practice common practice.

C H A P T E R   S U M M A R Y

This chapter has drawn together the idea of working together to provide the kind of effective mental health service that service users want and that will provide children with protection. Social workers can be involved as members of a team that responds to the needs of users including children. Children need to be more involved not just with their care and treatment but also should be consulted about service design and delivery. That they are not says more about our lack of imagination and faith than their abilities.

Child protection can never be far away from social work discourse and two Inquiries were considered to demonstrate what happens when things go wrong. Children also need to be recognised as potentially strong and resilient and the social work role might well be to enhance these strengths rather than concentrate on weaknesses. It is a reality that many children experience trauma and loss and work through this transition and emerge relatively unscathed.

Using the psychosocial model of intervention, various ways of working with parents were addressed and the advantage of this to social workers is that it allows us to make full use of a holistic view of mental disorder.

Clothier, C. (1994) The Allitt Inquiry considered the Beverly Allitt case, answering such questions as how she was allowed to qualify as a nurse, why her crimes were not detected sooner and what can be done to prevent another similar tragedy occurring in the future? The Inquiry also makes recommendations for changes in procedures.

Tony Newman and Sarah Blackburn (2002) of Barnardo's Policy, Research and Influencing Unit have produced a must-read paper that provides an in-depth examination of many of the issues raised in this chapter. It is called Transitions in the Lives of Children and Young People: Resilience Factors, published by the Scottish Executive Education Department and available electronically. www.scotland.gov.uk/publications

Quentin Spender et al. (2001) *Child Mental Health in Primary Care.* Abingdon: Radcliffe Medical Press is an excellent text that covers numerous child mental health problems and more. Includes check-lists and assessment questionnaires.

Every Child Matters sets out for consultation a framework for improving outcomes for all children and their families, to protect them, to promote their wellbeing and to support all children to develop their full potenial. DfES (2003) *Every Child Matters: The Next Steps* and *Every Child Matters: What You Said* (2004) Nottingham: DfES. Can be accessed at www.dfes.gov.uk/everychildmatters/

The booklet *Principles for Practice* (contains the Circle of Involvement ideas and more can be obtained from the Trent Multi Professional Deanery by emailing Rachel.Hawley@tsha.nhs.uk

Useful contacts

www.nhsdirect.nhs.uk

www.mind.org.uk

www.sane.org.uk

www.nsf.org.uk

www.doh.gov.uk/mentalhealth

www.bbc.co.uk/health/mental/

MACA (Mental Aftercare Association)
maca.bs@maca.org.uk
www.maca.org.uk

Parenting Plus
www.parentlineplus.org.uk

Winston's Wish
info@winstonswish.org.uk
www.winstonswish.org.uk

Social Care Institute for Excellence
www.scie.org.uk

Young Minds
enquiries@youngminds.org.uk
www.youngminds.org.uk

Lords Hansard
www.publication.parliament.uk

All JRF Findings are published on their website: www.jrf.org.uk

Glossary

Approved clinician (AC) This is an important new role that is not restricted to doctors and could include social workers. ACs have some of the powers that previously were reserved for doctors; this includes holding an inpatient for up to 72 hours in hospital to allow an application for assessment to be made.

Approved doctor under s.12 of the 1983 Mental Health Act A s.12 doctor is approved by the Secretary of State as *'having special experience in the diagnosis and treatment of mental disorder'*. Each region has its own selection panel, which sets standards for doctors who seek approval in their area.

Approved Mental Health Professional (AMHP) Section 118 of the MHA 2007 sees the role of the ASW replaced with the new role of AMHP. Only the AMHP or the nearest relative can make an application for compulsory admission. Unlike the ASW role, the AMHP may be drawn from a range of professionals, not doctors, but includes registered social workers, first-level nurses, occupational therapists or chartered psychologists.

Approved Social Worker (ASW) A qualified social worker who has undergone a 12-week additional training course. In order to comply with the 1983 Mental Health Act and ensure their independence, the ASW must be appointed and employed by the Local Social Services Department. Most ASW will transfer to the new role of Approved Mental Health Professional on the implementation date, which is expected to be October 2008. After this point the role of ASW will be of historical note only.

Behaviour modification Based on the idea of learning theory and conditioning. Intervention focuses on the relearning of behaviour.

Best Interest Assessors (BIA) This is a new role that provides an assessment to ensure that any act or decision made for or on behalf of a person who lacks capacity is made in their best interests.

BNF Stands for the **British National Formulary** reference text, which is published twice a year and contains up-to-date information about the maximum dosage of medication for patients. Hospital wards should always have the latest copy available.

Bolam test Where a healthcare professional is not considered to be negligent if s/he adopts the practice which a responsible body of professionals (e.g. psychiatrists, nurses or social workers) accept as appropriate.

CAMHS Child and Adolescent Mental Health Services.

CMHT Community Mental Health Team.

Cognitive therapy A treatment intervention, available on the NHS, that focuses on mal-adaptive patterns of thinking that affect the person's behaviour.

Commission for Social Care and Inspection and the Commission for Health, Audit and Inspection 2004 The National Care Standards Commission (NCSC) was the body that oversaw the commitment to health and social care standards in the independent sector, as set out in the **Care Standards Act (2000)**. The NCSC was established in April 2000 and abolished in April 2004 under the **Health and Social Care (Community Health and Standards) Act 2003 (HSCA)**.

The main body of the NCSC was merged with the Social Services Inspectorate **(SSI)** to form the **Commission for Social Care and Inspection**. The Private and Voluntary Healthcare Directorate (the department responsible for regulating all independent hospitals in England) combined with the Commission for Health Improvement and part of the Audit Commission to form **The Commission for Health, Audit and Inspection (CHAI)**. CHAI is now formally referred to as **The Healthcare Commission**.

Court of Protection Part VII of the 1983 Mental Health Act aims to protect the property and financial affairs of an individual who is incapable of acting because of a mental disorder. The MHA also provides safeguards for anyone authorised by the Court of Protection (Court) to manage the patient's finances.

CPN Community psychiatric nurses are qualified and experienced psychiatric nurses who play a major role in the supervision and treatment of patients in the community. Along with ASWs, psychiatrists and others, they have a pivotal role in community mental health and outreach teams.

CSIP NIMHE (National Institute of Mental Health for England) has now been absorbed into a successor body Care Services Improvement Partnership (CSIP). CSIP embraces eight programmes. They are the National Child and Adolescent Mental Health Services (CAMHS) Support Service; Health in Criminal Jusitice; the Integrated Care Network; Integrating Community Equipment and Support; the National Institute for Mental Health in England; the Health and Social Care Change Agent Team; the Valuing People Support Team; and Children for Change. It has an annual budget of more than £30 million. Chief executive: Richard Humphries. Website: www.csip.org.uk

Deprivation of liberty safeguards (DoLS) Section 50 of the MHA has amended the MCA 2005 to provide safeguards for those incapable people over 18 years of age that are deprived of liberty.

Diagnosis Forms part of the assessment process and the identification of specific mental disorder in which reference is made to either the **DSM IV** or to the **ICD–10** reference texts both of which classify mental disorder.

Expressed emotion This term is used usually in the sense that the family may have 'high expressed emotion' that is having a adverse effect on the service user. This includes over-involved parents and a highly critical atmosphere.

Family therapy The focus is on working with the family to restore the family system to a more functioning unit.

Home Office Mental Health Unit The Mental Health Unit was formerly known as C3 Division and it exercises the Home Secretary's powers in respect of restricted patients under the 1983 MHA.

HSC Health service circular.

HSG Health service guidance.

Independent Mental Capacity Advocates (IMCAs) provide a specialist advocacy service for people who lack capacity and who have no one, other than paid staff, to support them.

LA Local authority.

LAC Local Authority Circular.

LSSA Local Social Services Authority in England.

Mental Health Act (MHA) 1983 Although this legislation is over 20 years old it is still the primary legislation in this area. It is primarily about the compulsory admission, treatment and discharge of people who are diagnosed as having a mental disorder.

Mental Health Act (MHA) 2007 The main purpose of the 2007 Act is to admend the 1983 Act. It also introduces 'deprivation of liberty safeguards' through amending the Mental Capacity Act 2005 (MCA); supervised community treatment orders and extends the rights of victims by amending the Domestic Violence, Crime and Victims Act 2004. The main purpose of the legislation has been redefined to ensure that people with serious mental disorders and which threaten **either** their health or safety or the safety of the public can be treated even if they object if it is considered necessary to prevent them from harming themselves or others.

Mental Health Act Commission (MHAC) The Mental Health Act Commission (MHAC) is a Special Health Authority within the NHS. Commissioners are appointed by the Department of Health for a period to undertake this statutory role. The MHAC oversees the operation in respect of detained patients (see s.120 and s.121). The MHAC publishes a Biennial Report and a number of guidance notes on the interpretation of the various parts of the Act. Commissioners regularly visit all hospitals in England and Wales and meet with detained patients. The Health and Social Care Bill 2007 includes measures to abolish the present regulatory and inspection body known as the Mental Health Act Commission (MHAC) and transfer its functions (in relation to England) to the new Care Quality Commission which will provide an integrated approach to regulation of the sector. The expectation is that the Commission will be up and running in 2009 and fully operational by 2010.

Mental Health Act (MHA) hospital managers For the purposes of the 1983 Mental Health Act (MHA) it is important to differentiate between 'MHA managers' and any other hospital staff who may also be referred to as 'managers' in terms of a general management structure, e.g. a directorate manager or CMHT manager is not the 'MHA manager' in respect of the MHA. It is the 'MHA managers' who are the formal detaining authority under the Act, not the registered medical practitioner/responsible medical officer (RMO). At common law, 'the managers/NHS Trust' … are legally liable for any deprivation of liberty which is not justified by the Act.

Mental Health Act (MHA) Hospital Managers' Review Patients who are detained in hospital may request that the reasons for their continued detention in hospital are reviewed by the MHA hospital managers. The MHA hospital managers (s.23) can order the discharge of an unrestricted detained patient.

Mental Health Review Tribunal (MHRT) The Mental Health Review Tribunal (MHRT) is a court governed by the Lord Chancellor's Department. The purpose of the MHRT is to hear the patient's appeal against detention and reception into guardianship or supervised discharge can be made (see Part V of the MHA). The MHRT comprises three people: a legal member, lay member and medical member. The MHRT can order the discharge of a patient with or without conditions. It is now the case that in the case of civil partners, one will be the nearest relative of the other regardless of the time they have lived together.

National Institute for Clinical Excellence (NICE) Conducts research and evaluations of various treatments and publishes guidance and advice.

Nearest relative (NR) Clearly defined under s.26 of the MHA 1983.The nearest relative (NR) is usually, but not always, the patient's next-of-kin. Section 26 explains how to identify the NR. A common mnemonic is '**How Should Folk Be Graded, Give Us NewS**'. That is, **h**usband/wife; **s**on/daughter; **f**ather/mother; **b**rother/sister; **g**rand–parents; **g**randchild; **u**ncle/aunt; **n**ephew/niece; **s**ame sex partner. If the relatives are of equal standing, the eldest is preferred. In-laws are usually excluded. The patient cannot choose who the NR should be. It is now the case that in the case of civil partners, one will be the nearest relative of the other regardless of the time they have lived together.

National Institute of Mental Health England (NIMHE) See Care Services Improvement Partnership (CSIP).

NHS National Health Service.

Patient The term used throughout the MHA as is the male pronoun. Social workers use the term service user, implying more of a partnership exists between themselves and the 'user' of the service but patient is still used in the hospital setting.

The Mental Health Act 1983 provides that, unless otherwise stated and except in relation to the Court of Protection, the word *patient* means 'a person suffering or appearing to suffer from a mental disorder' (s.145(1)). In the context of tribunal proceedings, the patient is simply the person whose case is under review. There are a number of different types of patients, e.g. informal patients, voluntary patients and restricted patients.

PCT Primary Care Trust

PGO The Public Guardianship Office which is the executive agency based in the Lord Chancellor's office and which carries out the work of the Court of Protection.

PHCT Primary health care team.

Prognosis The medical assessment of the future course of events and probable outcome of the patient's mental disorder.

Psychoanalysis Based on Freud the aim is through the client/therapist relationship to resolve conflicted states of mind. Not available on the NHS.

Responsible Clinician (RC) This new role replaces the responsible medical officer (RMO) who until the Mental Health Act 2007 was the doctor who had full legal and clinical responsibility for a detained patient. Providing that the RC has already undertaken training as an AC, they need not be a doctor.

Responsible medical officer (RMO) The psychiatrist who has full clinical and legal responsibility for a patient detained under the 1983 Mental Health Act. Described within the 1983 MHA as the doctor who is in charge of the treatment of the patient. They will usually be a consultant psychiatrist and approved under s.12 of the MHA as having a special experience in the diagnosis and treatment of mental disorder. Due to be replaced by the RC.

Second opinion appointed doctor (SOAD) A registered medical practitioner (experienced psychiatrist) appointed by the MHAC to provide an independent opinion in respect of Consent to Treatment under Part IV of the 1983 Mental Health Act.

Section 12 approved doctor Approved by the Secretary of State as '... *having special experience in the diagnosis and treatment of mental disorder*'. Each strategic health authority/region has its own selection panel which sets standards for doctors who seek approval in their area, receives and scrutinises applications and grants approval under the 1983 MHA where appropriate.

SHA special health authority.

SSD Social services department.

Statutory A requirement dictated by Act of Parliament, e.g. the 1983 Mental Health Act.

Statutory duty A duty that must be complied with if contained within an Act of Parliament.

Statutory instrument Relates to delegated legislation drafted by the relevant department under powers attributed by an Act of Parliament. Statutory regulations are most commonly drafted as Statutory instruments and laid before Parliament, e.g. The Mental Health (Hospital, Guardianship and Consent to Treatment) Regulations 1983.

References

Ahmed, B. (1991) *Interpreters in Public Services* (eds Baker, P., Hussain, Z. and Saunders, J.). Birmingham: Venture Press.

Alcock, J. (2003) *Mental Health Services – Workforce design and development – best practice guidance*. London: DoH.

American Psychiatric Association (1994) *Diagnostic and Statistical Manual of Mental Disorders (DSM–IV)*. Washington DC: American Psychiatric Association.

Arnstein, S. (1969) A ladder of citizen participation in the USA. *Journal of the American Institute of Planners*, Vol 35, no 4.

Banks, S. (2002) *Ethics and Values in Social Work*. Basingstoke: Macmillan.

Bartlett, P. and Sandland, R. (2003) *Mental Health Law, Policy and Practice*. Oxford: Oxford University Press.

Bean, P. (1986) *Mental Disorder and Legal Control*. Cambridge: Cambridge University Press.

Bhopal, R. Spectre of racism in health and health care: lessons from history and the United States. *British Medical Journal*, 27 June 1998; 316: 1970–1973.

Blackburn, D. and Golightley, M. (2004) European Sociological Conference paper. University of Lincoln.

Bowers, L., Clark, N. and Callaghan, P. (2003). Multidisciplinary reflections on assessment for compulsory admission: the views of Approved Social Workers, general practitioners, ambulance crews, police, community psychiatric nurses and psychiatrists. *British Journal of Social Work*, Vol. 33,961–8.

Brammer, A. (2003) *Social Work Law*. Harlow: Pearson Educational.

Braye, S. Preston-Shoot, M. et al. (2005) *Teaching, Learning and Assessment of Law in Social Work Education*. Bristol: SCIE. Bristol: Policy Press.

Brock, A. and Griffiths, C. (2003) *Trends in the Mortality of Young Adults Aged 15–44 in England and Wales 1961–2001*. Office of National Statistics: Health Statistics Quarterly. See also website: www.statistics.gov.uk

Brown, G.W. and Harris, T.O. (1978) *The Social Origins of Depression*. London: Tavistock.

Brown, R. and Barber, P. (2008) *The Social Worker's Guide to Mental Capacity Law*. Exeter: Learning Matters.

Butler, A. and Pritchard, C. (1983) *Social Work and Mental Illness*. Basingstoke: Macmillan.

Campbell (1999) *Training for Mental Health 3: Exploring key areas*. Brighton: Pavilion Publishing.

Campbell, J. in K. O'Hagan (ed) *Competence in Social Work Practice: A practical guide for professionals*. London: Routledge, Kegan Paul.

Care Services Improvement (2006) *Reviewing the Care Programme Approach 2006: A consultation document*. London: CSI.

Carpenter, J., Schneider, J., Brandon, T. and Wooff, D. (2003) Working in multidisciplinary mental health teams: the impact on social workers and health professionals of integrated mental health care. *British Journal of Social Work*, 33, 1081–103.

Clark, C. (2000) *Social Work Ethics*. Basingstoke: Macmillan.

Clothier, C. (1994) *Report of the Inquiry into Beverley Allit: The Allit Inquiry* (1991). London: HMSO.

Cochrane, R. (1983) *The Social Creation of Mental Illness*. London: Longman Applied Psychology.

Coid, J.W. (1996) Dangerous patients with mental illness; increased risks warrant new policies, adequate resources, and appropriate legislation. *British Medical Journal* 312: 965–6.

Crawford, K. and Walker, J. (2003) *Social Work and Human Development*. Exeter: Learning Matters.

Cree, V. (2002) The changing nature of social work in R. Adams et al. (eds) *Social Work: Themes, issues and critical debates*. Basingstoke: Palgrave.

Curran, C. and Bingley, W. (2003) Seclusion: Part 1 3, *Openmind*, Nov/Dec, No 124, p.29.

Curran, C. and Grimshaw, C. (1996) Supervised discharge. *Openmind* Sept/Oct, No 81, p.28.

Curran, C. and Grimshaw, C. (1998) The use of Guardianship under the 1983 Mental Health Act. *Openmind*, Sept/Oct, No 93, p.24.

Curran, C. and Grimshaw, C. (2000) Advocacy in mental health. *Openmind*, Jan/Feb, No 101, p.24.

Curran, C. and Grimshaw, C. (2000) Consent to treatment for medication under the 1983 Mental Health Act. *Openmind*, March/April, No 102, pp.24–5.

Curran, C. and Grimshaw, C. (2000) Mental Health Review Tribunals. *Openmind*, May/June, No 103, p.24.

Curran, C. and Grimshaw, C. (2000) The Mental Health Unit at the Home Office. *Openmind*, July/Aug, No 104, p.24.

Curran, C. and Grimshaw, C. (2000) Review of treatment under s.61 of the Mental Health Act 1983. *Openmind*, Sept/Oct, No 105, p.24.

Curran, C. and Grimshaw, C. (2000) Review of treatment under s.61 of the Mental Health Act 1983 revised. *Openmind*, Nov/Dec, No 106, p.24.

Curran, C. and Grimshaw, C. (2001) Police holding power under s.136 of the 1983 Mental Health Act. *Openmind*, Jan/Feb, No 107, p.24.

Curran, C. and Grimshaw, C. (2001) Leave of absence under s.17 of the 1983 Mental Health Act. *Openmind*, Nov/Dec, No 112, p.24.

Curran, C. and Grimshaw. C. (2002) Compulsory admission to an NHS or independent hospital, *Openmind*, Jan/Feb, No113, p.29.

Curran, C. and Grimshaw. C. (2002) Information for patients detained under the 1983 Mental Health Act. *Openmind*, Jan/Feb No 119, p.29.

Curran, C. and Grimshaw. C. (2002) The Role of the RMO under the 1983 Mental Health Act. *Openmind*, July/Aug, No 116, p.29.

Curran, C. and Grimshaw. C. (2002) The Court of Protection patients. *Openmind*, Sept/Oct No 117, p.29.

Curran, C. and Grimshaw. C. (2002) Doctors approved under s.12 of the 1983 Mental Health Act. *Openmind*, Nov/Dec No 118, p.29.

Curran, C. and Grimshaw, C. (2003) Detention of patients under Part III of the 1983 Mental Health Act. *Openmind*, March/April No 120, p.29.

Curran, C. and Grimshaw, C. (2003) Warrant to search and remove patients under s.135 of the 1983 Mental Health Act. *Openmind*, July/Aug No 122, p.29.

Curran, C. and Grimshaw, C. (2004) Seclusion part 2. *Openmind*, March/April No 126.

Curran, C. and Grimshaw, C. (2004) Guide to the Mental Capacity Bill 2003. *Openmind*, July.

Curran, C. and Grimshaw, C. (2007) Independent Mental Capacity Advocates under the Mental Capacity Act 2005 Part I and Part II. *Openmind*, No. 150, 24–5.

Curran, C. Grimshaw, C. and Hewitt, C. (1999) The Nearest Relative Under the 1983 Mental Health Act. *Openmind* May/June, No 97, p.24.

Curran, C., Grimshaw, C. and Hewitt, D. (1999) The 1983 Mental Health Act Revised Code of Practice: Some implications for Approved Social Workers. *Community Care* 8 July, pp. 28–9.

Curran, C., Grimshaw, C. and Hewitt, D. (2001) The Human Rights Act and mental health law. *Openmind*, May/June, No 109, pp.24–5.

Curran, C., Grimshaw, C. and Zigmond, A. (1997) The doctor's holding power under section 5(2) *Openmind* No 83, p.28.

Curran, C. and Hewitt, D. (2002) National Care Standards Commission and independent psychiatric hospitals. *Openmind*, March/April, No 114, pp. 28–9.

Dein , S. (1997), Clinical review. ABC of mental health: mental health in a multiethnic society, *British Medical Journal*.

Department for Constitutional Affairs (2007) *Mental Capacity Act 2005 Code of Practice*. Issued by the Lord Chancellor on 23 April 2007 in accordance with sections 42 and 43 of the Act. London: TSO.

Department of Health (1990) *National Health Service and Community Care Act*. London: DoH.

Department of Health (1993) *The Health of the Nation: A strategy for health in England*. London: HMSO.

Department of Health (1995) *Building Bridges Report*. London: DoH.

Department of Health (1995) *A Handbook on Child and Adolescent Mental Health*. London: HMSO.

Department of Health (1998) *Modernising Mental Health Services: National Priorities Guidance 1999/00–2001/02* LAC(98)22.

Department of Health (1998) *Modernising Mental Health Services: Safe, sound and supportive*. London: DoH.

Department of Health (1998) *Partnerships in Action: New opportunities for joint working between health and social services: a discussion document*. London: DoH.

Department of Health (1999) *Code of Practice to the Mental Health Act 1983 (revised 1999)*. Norwich: Stationery Office.

Department of Health (1999) *National Service Framework for Mental Health – Modern Standards and Service Models*. London: DoH.

Department of Health (1999) *Quality Protects Programme: Transforming children's services 2000–01* LAC (99) 33, London: HMSO.

Department of Health (1999) *The Mental Health Act 1983 Revised Code of Practice*, London: DoH.

Department of Health (1999) *Safer Services: National confidential inquiry into suicide and homicide by people with mental illness*. London: DoH.

Department of Health (2000) *The NHS Plan: a plan for investment: a plan for reform.* London:HMSO.

Department of Health (2001) *Safeguarding Children in Whom Illness is Induced or Fabricated by Carers with Parenting Responsibilities*. London: HMSO.

Department of Health (2001) *Treatment Choice in Psychological Therapies and Counselling: Evidence based clinical practice guidelines*. London: DoH.

Department of Health (2001) *Valuing People: A new strategy for learning disability for the 21st century*. London: TSO.

Department of Health (2002) *A Sign of the Times: Modernising mental health services for people who are deaf*. London: DoH.

Department of Health (2002) *Dual Diagnosis Good Practice Guide*. London: TSO.

Department of Health (2002) *Mental Health Implementation Guide: Dual diagnosis good practice guide*. London: DoH.

Department of Health (2001) *The Mental Health Policy Implementation Guide*. London: DoH.

Department of Health (2003) *Delivering Race Equality: A framework for Action*. Consultation Document. London: DoH.

Department of Health (1999) *Effective Care Co-Ordination in Mental Health Services: Modernising the Care Programme Approach – a policy booklet*. London: DoH.

Department of Health (2003) *Skills for Health*. London: DoH.

Department of Health (2003) *Women's Mental Health: Into the mainstream: strategic development of mental health care for women*. London: DoH.

Department of Health (2004) *An Easy Guide to Direct Payments*. London: TSO.

Department of Health, (2006), White Paper – Our health, our care, our say: A new direction for community services. 30 January.

Department of Health (2004) Core Document, National Service Framework for Children, Young People and Maternity Services.

Department of Health (2006) *Mental Health Bill 2006: Regulatory impact assessment*. London: Department of Health.

Department of Health (2007) *Mental Health Bill: Amending the Mental Health Act 1983* London: Department of Health.

Department of Health (2007) MHA 2007 Overview Nov 2007. accessed January 29 www.dh.gov.uk/en/policyandguidance/Heathandsocialcare topics/Mental health

Department of Health (2007) *Mental Health Act 1983 Draft Revised Code of Practice* (2007) Para 4.4. London: DoH.

Department of Health (2008) *Refocusing the Care Programme Approach: Best Practice Guidance*. London: DoH.

Dogra, N., Parkin, A., Gale, F. and Frake, C.(2001) *A Multidisciplinary Handbook of Child and Adolescent Mental Health for Front Line Professionals*. London: Jessica Kingsley.

Dominelli, L, (1988) *Anti–Racist Social Work. A challenge for white practitioners and educators*. Basingstoke: Macmillan.

Double D, (2006) *Critical Psychiarty: Limits of Madness*, New York. Palgrave Macmillan.

Eastman N, (1995) Antitherapeutic community mental health law. *British Medical Journal*, vol. 310, 1081–2.

European Commission (2005) Green Paper – Improving the mental health of the population: Towards a strategy on mental health for the European Union.

Eldergill, A. (1997) *Mental Health Law Review Tribunals: Law and practice*. Sweet and Maxwell: London.

Epstein, S. (1983) Natural healing processes of the mind, in J. Newton (1988), *Preventing Mental Illness*, London: Routledge.

Fennell, P. (2007) *Mental Health: The new law*. Bristol: Jordan Publishing.

Fernado, S. Ethnicity and Mental Health in M. Ulas, and A. Connor (1999) *Mental Health and Social Work*. London: Jessica Kinglsey.

Findings (2004) Understanding What Children Say About Living with Domestic Violence, Parental Substance Misuse or Parental Health Problems. York: JRF.

Finzen, A. (2002) in S. Priebe, and M. Slade *Evidence in Mental Health Care*. Hove: Brunner-Routledge.

Fox, C. and Hawton, K. (2004) *Deliberate Self-Harm in Adolescence*. London: Jessica Kingsley.

Frangou, S. and Bryne, P. (2000) How to manage the first episode of schizophrenia. *British Medical Journal* 321 (7260):522.

Fulford, K.W.M. (2004a), Ten principles of values-based practice (VBP), in Radden (ed.) *Companion to the Philosophy of Psychiatry*. New York: Oxford University Press.

Fulford, K.W.M. (2004b) Values in Mental Health Services, in Mental Health Act Commission Tenth Biennial Report 2001–3. Norwich: Stationery Office.

Gilbert, P. (2003), *The Value of Everything: Social work and its importance in the field of mental health*. Lyme Regis: Russell House Publishing.

Glover, K. in T. Bassett and S. Cuthbert (2000) *Certificate in Community Mental Health*. Student's workbook. Southampton: Ashford Press.

Goffman, E. (1961) *Asylums*. London: Penguin.

Golightley, T.M. (1985) *If Only They Would Listen: The case for a community orientated mental health service*. Lincoln: University of Lincoln.

Gomm, R. (2004) *Social Research Methodology: critical introduction*. Basingstoke: Palgrave Macmillan.

Gottlieb, B. (ed) (1981) *Social Networks and Social Support*. London: Sage.

Gould, M. (2008) Will community treatment orders work? *Health Service Journal* accessed 23 March 2008 from www.hsj.co.uk/insideknowledge/2008/01/will_community_treatment_orders_ work.html

Griffiths, R. (1988) *Community Care: Agenda for Action*. London: HMSO.

GSCC (2002) *Codes of Practice for Social Care Workers and Employers*. London: General Social Care Council.

Health Advisory Service (1994) *Suicide Prevention: The challenge confronted*. London: HMSO.

Health Advisory Service (1995) *Child and Adolescent Mental Health Services – Together We Stand*. London: HMSO.

Health Advisory Service (2001) *Substance Misuse and Mental Health Comorbity (Dual Diagnosis): Standards for Mental Health Services*. London: HAS.

Hewitt, D. (2005) An inconvenient mirror – do we already have the next Mental Health Act. *Journal of Mental Health Law* November pp. 138–49.

Hewitt, D. (2007) *The Nearest Relative Handbook*. London: Jessica Kingsley.

Horner, N. (2003) *What is Social Work? Context and perspectives*. Exeter: Learning Matters.

Huxley, P. (1985) *Social Work Practice in Mental Health*. Aldershot: Gower.

Huxley, P. (2002) Evidence in social care, in S. Priebe and M. Slade, *Evidence in Mental Health Care*. Hove: Brunner-Routledge.

James, J. (2003) *Seeing Through Walls: A report on social inclusion in practice based on the findings of the Social Inclusion Mapping Exercise*. Durham: Northern Centre for Mental Health.

Johns, R. (2003) *Using the Law in Social Work*. Exeter; Learning Matters.

Jones, K. (1993) *Asylums and After: A revised history of the mental health services from the early 18th century to the 1900s*. London: Athlone Press.

Jones, K. et al. (1985) *After Hospital: A study of long term psychiatric patients in York*. York: York District Health Authority.

Jones, R. (2002) *Mental Health Act Manual* (8th ed). London: Sweet and Maxwell.

Joseph Rowntree Foundation (2004) *Mental Health Service Users and their Involvement in Risk Assessment and Management*. York: JRF ref. 414.

Kalfi, Y. and Torabi, M. (1996) The Role of Parental 'Expressed Emotion' in Relapse of Schizophrenia. *Iran Journal of Medicine*: 21(1 72): 46.

Keating, F. and Robertson, D. (2002) Breaking the circles of fear: a review of mental health services to African and Caribbean communities, in *Your Shout: Mental Health Promotion*, Issue 4. pp. 18–19.

Kim, W.J. (1995) A training guideline of cultural competence for child and adolescent psychiatric residencies. *Child Psychiatry and Human Development* 26:2, 125–36.

Kreitman, N. (1997) *Parasuicide*. Chichester: Wiley.

Laing, R.D. (1985) *Wisdom, madness and folly. The making of a psychiatrist*. Basingstoke: Macmillan.

Langan, J. and Lindow, V. (2004) *Living with Risk: Mental health service user involvement in risk assessment and management*. Bristol: Policy Press.

Leff, J., Kuipers, K. and Lam, D. (2002) *Family Work for Schizophrenia* (2nd ed). London: Royal College of Psychiatrists.

Low, J. (2004) *Lay acquiescence to medical dominance in assessing the efficacy of alternative and complementary therapies: reflections on the active citizenship thesis*. Paper presented to the European Sociological Association Symposium on Professions, Social Inclusion and Citizenship. Lincoln: University of Lincoln.

MacLean, M. (2004) *Together and Apart: Children and parents experiencing divorce*. York: JRF (Foundations series).

Mckeown, M. and Mercer, D. (1998) Language, race and forensic psychiatry, in T. Mason, and C. Mercer, (eds) *Critical Perspectives in Forensic Care*. Basingstoke: Macmillan.

Menninger, K. (1963) *The Vital Balance: The life process in mental health and illness*. London: Viking Press.

Mental Capacity Act Code of Practice (2007) London: The Stationery Office.

Mental Health Act Commission (MHAC) (1998) Written submission to House of Lords. In Shaw, I., Middleton, H. and Cohen, J. (2007) *Understanding Treatment without Consent*. Aldershot: Ashgate.

Mental Health Act Commission (1999–2001) *Ninth Biennial Report*. London: Stationery Office.

Mental Health Foundation (1999) *The Big Picture: Promoting children and young people's mental health*. London: Mental Health Foundation.

Mischon, J. (2000) Report of the independent inquiry team into the care and treatment of Daniel Joseph. Sutton and Wandsworth Health Authority and Lambeth, Southwark and Lewisham Health Authority.

Modestein and Schwarzenbach (1992) Effect of psycho–pharmacotherapy on suicide risk in discharged psychiatric patients, Acta Psychiatrica Scandinavia in C. Pritchard (1995) *Suicide – The Ultimate Rejection*. Buckingham: Open University Press.

Nazroo, J. (1999) *Ethnicity and Mental Health*. London: Policy Studies Institute.

Neustatter, A. (2003) Changing shapes, in *Young Minds Magazine*, No 68 .

Newman, T. and Blackburn, S. (2002) *Transitions in the Lives of Children and Young People: Resilience factors*. Barnardo's Policy, Research and Influencing Unit: Scottish Executive Education Department.

Newton, J. (1988) *Preventing Mental Illness*. London: Routledge.

NIMHE, (2003) Inside outside: improving mental health services for black and minority ethnic communities in England. www.nimhe.org.uk

NIMHE, (2006) National Suicide Prevention Strategy for England: Annual Report on Progress 2005, Care Service Improvement Partnership, Leeds.

O'Hagan, K. (ed) (1996) *Competence in Social Work Practice*. London: Jessica Kingsley.

O'Sullivan, T. (1999) *Decision Making in Social Work*. Basingstoke: Macmillan.

Obafunwa, J.O. and Busuttil, A. (1994) Clinical contact preceding suicide, in C. Pritchard (1995) *Suicide – The Ultimate Rejection*. Buckingham: Open University Press.

Oliver, M. (1996) *Understanding Disability: from theory to practice*. Basingstoke: Macmillan.

Onyett, S. (1992) *Case Management in Mental Health*. Cheltenham: Stanley Thornes.

Orbach, S. (1986) *Hunger Strike*. London: Penguin.

Our Health, our care, our say: A new direction for community services. White Paper accessible at www.dh.gov.uk/ourhealthourcareoursay

Parker, J. and Bradley, G. (2003) *Social Work Practice: Assessment, planning, intervention and review*. Exeter: Learning Matters.

Patel, K. et al. (2003) *Engaging and Changing: Developing effective policy for the care and treatment of black and minority ethnic detained patients*. London: DoH.

Pearce, J. (1999) Collaboration between the NHS and Social Services in the provision of child and adolescent mental health services: a personal view. *Child Psychology and Psychiatry Review*, 4;4, 150–3.

Pharoah F. M., Mari, J. J. and Steiner, D. (2000) *American Journal of Psychiatry*, 153, 607–17 in the Cochrane Library issue 3, 2002, Oxford update software.

Pilgrim, D. and Rogers, A. (1999) *A Sociology of Mental Health and Illness* (2nd ed). Buckingham: Open University Press.

Pollack, W. (1999) *Real Boys*. New York: Henry Holt.

Poole, D.L. (1998) Politically correct or culturally competent, *Health and Social Work*, 23 (3) 163–6.

Priebe, S. and Slade, M. (2002) *Evidence in Mental Health Care*. Hove: Brunner-Routledge.

Prins, H. (1999) *Will They Do It Again?: Risk assessment and management in criminal justice and psychiatry*. London: Routledge.

Pritchard, C. (1995) *Suicide – The Ultimate Rejection*. Buckingham: Open University Press.

Ramon, S. (2001) Opinions and dilemmas facing British mental health social work, in J. Tew, Going social: championing a holistic model of mental distress within professional education, *Social Work Education*, Vol 21 No 2, 2002.

Red Manual Code of Practice (2004) *Section D:10 working with parents with mental health problems*. Lincoln: Lincolnshire County Council.

Rethink, Sane and Zito Trust (2003) Behind Closed Doors: The current state and future of acute mental health care in the UK. London: *Rethink*. www.rethink.org/research/Behind-Closed/Doors.htm

Ridgeway, S.M. (1997) Deaf people and psychological health – some preliminary findings. *Deaf Worlds*, Issue 1, Vol 13, 9–17.

Rikken, M. (1995) A preventive mental health programme for children of parents with mental disorders, in D. Trent, and A. Reed (1995) *Promotion of Mental Health*. Aldershot: Ashgate.

Ritchie, J.H., Dick D. and Lingham, R. (1994) *The Report of the Inquiry into the Care and Treatment of Christopher Clunis*. London: HMSO.

Robbins, D. (2004) *Treated as People: An overview of mental health services from a social care perspective*. London: SSI/DoH.

Rodgers, B. and Pryor, J. (1998) *Divorce and Separation: The outcome for children*. York: JRF.

Rowland, N. and Gross, S. (2003) *Evidence-Based Counselling and Psychological Therapies*. Hove: Brunner-Routledge.

Rutter, M. (1999) *Bright Futures: Promoting children and young people's mental health*. London: Mental Health Foundation.

Sainsbury Centre for Mental Health (1998) *Keys to Engagement: review of care for people with severe mental illness who are hard to engage with services*. London: Sainsbury Centre.

Sainsbury Centre for Mental Health (2002) *Breaking the Circles of Fear*. London: Sainsbury Centre.

Sainsbury Centre for Mental Health (2003) *Mental Health Topics: Assertive outreach*. London: Sainsbury Centre.

Sartorius, N. et al. (1990) *Sources and Traditions of Classification in Psychiatry*. World Health Organisation/Hogrefe and Huber. Toronto: Lewiston.

Schram, A. et al. (1999) *Positive Practice in Mental Health* (2nd ed). Crook: Breakthrough.

Scull, A.T. (1979) *Museums of Madness: The social organisation of insanity in 19th century England*. London: Allen Lane.

Spender, Q. et al. (2001) *Child Mental Health in Primary Care*. Abingdon: Radcliffe Medical Press.

Swinton J (2001) *Spirituality and Mental Health Care*. London: Jessica Kingsley

Szasz, T.S. (1972) *The myth of mental illness*. London: Paladin.

Tew, J. (2002) Going social: championing a holistic model of mental distress within professional education. *Social Work Education*, Vol. 21, no. 2.

Trent D. and Reed, C. (eds) (1995) *Promotion of Mental Health Vol. 4* Aldershot: Avebury.

Trent NHS Strategic Health Authority. (2005) Principles for Practice. December. Available by email request from Rachel.Hawley@tsha.nhs.uk

Tribe, R. and Raval, H. (eds) (2003) *Working with Interpreters in Mental Health*. Hove: Brunner-Routledge.

Ulas, M. and Connor, A. (1999) *Mental Health and Social Work Research Highlights in Social Work 28*. London: Jessica Kingsley .

Walker, S. (2003) *Social Work and Child and Adolescent Mental Health*. Lyme Regis: Russell House Publishing.

Walker, S. (2003) Social work and child mental health: psychological principles in community practice. *British Journal of Social Work* 33: 673–87.

Walker, S. (2003) *Working Together for Healthy Young Minds*. Lyme Regis: Russell House Publishing.

Webb, S. (2006) *Social Work in a Risk Society*. New York: Palgrave Macmillan.

Webster, R. (1996) *Why Freud Was Wrong: Science, sin and psychoanalysis*, London: HarperCollins.

Weal, A. (1999) *Adolescence: Positive approaches for working with young people*. Lyme Regis: Russell House Publishing.

WHO (2001) World Health Report, p11.http://www.who.int/whr/2001

Williams, R. and Morgan, G. (eds) (1994) *Suicide Prevention: The challenge confronted*. London: HMSO.

Yelloly, M.A. (1980) *Social Work Theory and Psychoanalysis*. Wokingham: Van Nostrand Rheinhold.

Index